Collins Field Notebook of
BRITISH BIRDS

Text by
Roger Lovegrove

Illustrations by
Philip Snow

Collins 8 Grafton Street   London W1

Author's Acknowledgements

The art – is it not nowadays a science? – of the field identification of birds has reached levels of skill in Britain which were probably undreamed of years ago. I would like to acknowledge that such skill now exists – and continues to develop yet further – and that I have been particularly able to draw on it through the help of my friend John McLoughlin. He has painstakingly commented on all the texts and his thoughts and suggestions have been invaluable. In addition, I would record my grateful thanks to several other colleagues who have generously commented on individual groups in which they have special knowledge: Tony Prater (waders), Rob Hume (gulls and terns) and Graham Burton (wildfowl).

Valerie Rushton and Marion Jones produced typescripts, often at impossibly short notice but still with unwavering accuracy.

Most of all, I express my thanks to Ingola for her support and understanding throughout the spring and summer of 1985; as ever, it would have been impossible to produce this book without her, and for that I am deeply grateful.

Roger Lovegrove, September 1985

Artist's Acknowledgements

My sincere thanks are due to all those who kindly looked at, and commented on, my artwork, especially John McLoughlin, and also Graham Williams, Graham Burton – and, of course, Roger and Ingola.

Thanks are also due to all those who have inspired me, directly or indirectly, including Charles Tunnicliffe, Lars Jonsson, Bruno Liljefors, Raymond Ching and George McLean: and Miles Davis, Pat Metheny, Gustav Mahler, Laurens Van der Post, Ralf and Maraji.

Philip Snow, September 1985

William Collins Sons & Co Ltd
London Glasgow Sydney Auckland
Toronto Johannesburg

First published 1986
This edition planned and produced by Robert MacDonald Publishing

ISBN 0 00 219175 X

Colour reproduction by Adroit Photolitho Ltd, Birmingham
Typeset by Wordsmiths Graphics Ltd, London

Made and printed in Great Britain by
William Collins Sons & Co Ltd, Glasgow

Contents

Bird watching has much to commend it. It requires no expensive equipment; it can be undertaken literally almost anywhere at any time, both in town and country; it requires no predetermined level of skill; it can be enjoyed by anyone at whatever level of proficiency they set themselves. Moreover, it is an activity that lends itself to enjoyment either solo or in a family or larger group. Because you can watch birds through a kitchen window or a car windscreen, it does not exclude the physically handicapped, nor commit the less intrepid birdwatcher to the discomforts of inclement weather. Birdwatching is for everybody!

We hope that this book will be of particular help to those, whether young or old, who are taking an interest in birds for the first time, or those who have been birdwatching for a while but who do not yet profess a high level of skill. It has been designed to introduce you to some of the rules, knacks and disciplines of birdwatching, which are essential both to greater proficiency and to the full enjoyment of one of the most pleasurable of all pastimes.

About this book.

This book has been designed with the British, rather than the European birdwatcher in mind, and it has been both written and illustrated specifically to be of most use to the birdwatcher in the field. It covers some 280 species of British birds – essentially those which are of most regular occurrence. It therefore includes all those species which either breed habitually (even if only a few pairs), or occur annually as winter visitors, or pass through the British Isles regularly on migrations to and from their more northerly breeding grounds. The great majority of birds in the book are therefore species that can be seen by a birdwatcher with reasonable experience and diligence (and quite a lot of time) in the course of a year, should he or she so wish. A few (White Stork, Crane, Ortolan Bunting, Hoopoe or Melodious Warbler, for example) require a larger slice of luck and cannot safely be predicted in the course of any one year. The book does not attempt to embrace the increasingly long list of rarities which occur as haphazard or isolated vagrants each year.

The listing of species broadly follows the conventional (Voous) order (which is that used in the British Trust for Ornithology checklist included with the book). However, there are a number of departures from the strict order set out by Voous; these are generally to allow us to deal with 'like species' on a single page or, in other instances, to group together a restricted number of birds that are likely to be seen in one particular habitat. Thus Gannet, Storm Petrel and Cormorant, though widely separated in the checklist, are all most likely to be seen at sea, and have therefore all been illustrated on one page (Seabirds at Sea, pp. 64-65). Similarly Reed Warbler, Bearded Tit and Reed Bunting – all small birds of reed-beds and reed-bed margins – will be found under Marsh Warblers and Allies on pp. 106-107. Species within large groups may also not follow established order. Thus ducks are divided here more by habitat and habits (Diving Freshwater Ducks, pp. 32-33; Grazing Freshwater Ducks, pp. 30-31; Dabbling Ducks, pp. 28-29;

INTRODUCTION

for example) than by closeness of relationship: in this way, two such species as Red-breasted Merganser and Goosander, although closely related and basically similar, are dealt with on different pages because they are nearly always found in different types of habitat. Conversely, the Crane appears on the same page as other long-legged birds such as the Heron because this enables us to point out the ways in which it can be distinguished from the other birds with which it is most likely to be confused. In one or two cases – for example, on pages 84-85 and 94-95, species which are the only representatives of their families to occur in Britain (Dipper, Treecreeper, Golden Oriole, Nightjar, Cuckoo and others) are grouped together on one page purely for reasons of convenience and expediency. For the relatively inexperienced birdwatcher, who may only be sure of the size and colour of the bird he is studying, and of the habitat it is in, the 'quick reference' index on the back flap of the book (opposite the note pad) will probably provide the best method of finding the relevant pages in the book.

Scientific names of species have not been used in the main text, nor in the captions to the illustrations: those who wish to refer to them will find them alongside the English names in the index. Except in those few instances where both main species description and illustration and text occur on the same page (for example Swans, p. 23, and Skuas, p. 71) all illustrations are on the left hand page, facing the principal descriptive texts, so that the birdwatcher can use the note pad and refer to the illustrations simultaneously. These texts are complementary to the smaller caption descriptions accompanying the individual pictures. When attempting to confirm an identification, use both main text and caption text, as well as the illustrations themselves. In many cases, obvious plumage features are not spelled out in words as they are assumed to be evident from the illustrations.

The illustrations
Throughout the book, we have attempted to represent each species in attitudes or poses in which they are likely to be seen in the field, rather than to produce a series of more artificial 'portrait' poses. Accordingly, many groups (birds of prey, gulls, skuas and other seabirds) are principally shown in flight, as this is the context in which they are most often seen. For similar reasons, divers and grebes are illustrated on water, chats are shown perched, tits feeding, and ducks in flight as well as on land and water. At the same time, we have included, for all species, as many flight illustrations as space has allowed. In these ways, we hope that the artist's skill will be able to convey some of that almost indefinable quality of 'jizz' – a personal interpretation of the appearance, the 'feel', the movements, shape, attitude and manner of a bird, often impossible to explain or put into a form of words, and not related to colour or pattern, but which confirms the recognition of a bird for us without our necessarily being able to say exactly why it is so.

A second major feature of the illustrations is that we have consciously tried to avoid falling into the trap of invariably showing the male adult in full breeding plumage as the principal illustration. In many cases, it is, of course right to do so, and to relate other age/sex/seasonal plumages to it (Stonechat, Hen Harrier and Mandarin Duck, for example). But most of us will never see Grey Phalarope, Ruff, Spotted Redshank, Little Gull or Lapland Bunting – among others – in full breeding plumage in Britain, and it is much more useful and less misleading – despite the temptations of brightly coloured plumage – to portray such species in the drabber plumages in which they are likely to be seen in this country.

The Note Pad

The note pad at the back of the book is inserted in such a way that it can be placed over the right hand page of the guide book, wherever the book is open, so that it faces the illustrations. This important feature of the Field Notebook is particularly designed to encourage the careful describing and recording of observations. There are two good reasons why this should be done.

First, the sketching of birds seen in the field, together with relevant notes about an observation (date, time, place, habitat, weather and visibility, activity and so on) is fundamental to any serious attempt to acquire the essential accuracy and detail required for bird identification. It is probably fair to say that only in this way are you likely to be sufficiently careful and perceptive in detailing the important points of an interesting observation or a new identification. The design of this book, dovetailed as it is with the artist's style of painting, is intended to promote this practice and thereby aid careful recording and observation.

Second, it should be a part of any birdwatcher's responsibility to ensure that records of interest or significance are passed on to the relevant recorders (normally county recorders, a list of whom is available from the B.T.O. – see p. 15 and Checklist for details), because many records have genuine scientific, conservation or other interest and should be duly reported and possibly published. Such records usually need to be substantiated by notes and/or sketches made at the time, and we hope that the provision of a note pad with this book will encourage the development of this habit as standard practice right from the start.

The Checklist

A copy of the British Trust for Ornithology standard checklist is included in the pocket at the back of the book. It includes all species that have been seen on at least five occasions per year, on average, in the British Isles in recent years (differing therefore, in minor respects, from the list of species illustrated in the guide). This is an invaluable and popular list which can be used in several ways to help you record what birds you have seen. Use a single column to keep a record of a particular day's outing, or as a checklist for the garden, your favourite local birdwatching spot, a holiday trip or for any similar purpose. Once again, there is value in the discipline required in methodical recording of this sort. Author, artist and publisher are indebted to the B.T.O. for their generosity in supplying the material for inclusion in this book.

IDENTIFYING BIRDS

Nobody should pretend that bird identification is easy. Nevertheless, everybody has some point from which to start, however lowly it may be. There are few people who do not genuinely recognise a Robin, Mute Swan, House Sparrow or Blackbird. Most can tell a Blue Tit from a thrush and a Kingfisher from a Heron. At the other extreme, birdwatching can be sufficiently sophisticated for the age, sex and origin of an individual bird to be identifiable at a couple of hundred yards. There is pleasure to be had from watching birds at either level, and at all levels in between, but you will certainly find that your enjoyment of birdwatching grows with your skill at identification and the devlopment of these skills will be amply rewarded.

In the early stages, the inexperienced birdwatcher is likely to rely on size, shape and colour to identify a bird, usually with the aid of an illustration in a book. As your skill grows, you will come to recognise other factors that are also important. It is worth considering some of these in the context of this book.

Size

Size is obviously fundamental. We have not given measurements for each species, since it is often difficult, if not impossible, to relate *absolute* size to a distant view of a bird in the field. Much more important is *relative* size, and this is what we have tried to suggest throughout the book. Thus, on page 102 for example, oak leaves should suggest the size of the Wood Warbler, just as, on page 38, the Moorhen prey does for the Marsh Harrier (and thereby the other harriers on the page). In some cases, subsidiary illustrations of unrelated but more familiar species have been included specifically to provide comparisons of size. On each individual page, the principal illustrations of the different species are, in nearly every case, in scale with each other. Any variation in scale is indicated in the caption to the illustration.

Voice

For many species, the most important single feature determining identification is voice. It soon becomes apparent to every aspiring birdwatcher that birds do not always place themselves in view at close range, thus conveniently allowing visual identification. Learning to identify the songs and calls of birds opens a vast new field of recognition. Such learning is not always easy, however, and there is no substitute for being taken out in the field by someone who already knows bird songs and calls: even then, the process is not a fast one.

In a field guide such as this, there are inherent problems in trying to render bird songs and calls on paper. What we have tried to do is to represent the most important aspects of voice for all those species where it is genuinely helpful; sometimes it is the song, at other times contact calls (as for the Redwing) or alarm calls (Blackbird), that are most important. Rendering such avian sounds in print is probably the least successful part of any field guide: apart from anything else, the range of calls that can emanate from a single species can itself be astonishingly wide and complex. To walk through a woodland in July or August and hear the baffling range of thin "seeping" calls from young birds of many species is to get some idea of the complexity of the subject. Do not be put off, however! Build on the obvious beginnings of Cuckoo, Blackbird, Robin or Rook, and the rest will slowly follow.

Distribution

We have tried to give for each species a reasonable summary of where and when it is most likely to be seen in Britain. Where the distribution in Ireland is significant (particularly in those cases where a species is absent from Ireland altogether), details have been given in the text. Information about distribution can obviously be critical in helping to establish an identification. Birds may always contrive to confound us, producing a Swallow in December or a Gannet far inland, but these are the oddities, and an understanding of the more normal habitat preferences and seasonal and geographical distributions within the British Isles is important. By such means, a suspected sighting of a phalarope in winter, Eider on the south coast or a Twite on Dartmoor in May can probably be quickly discounted. We hope that the text gives genuine guidance in this direction.

Plumage detail

Finally, a word about plumages. A small portable guide such as this, covering a large number of species in a small space, is necessarily selective and thereby restricted in what it can include. Many bird species do in fact have a far greater range of plumages than can be described and illustrated in one small volume. Not only are there male and female, winter and summer plumages, but also a host of transitional plumages, juveniles and immatures – often in several stages – and regional differences (for example the Guillemot, which is dark brown in the south of Britain and gets blacker the further north you go). To give full details of these would be beyond the scope of this book, and a catalogue of numerous fine differences would anyway be more confusing than helpful in the field. In this book, therefore, we have concentrated on the 'major' plumages – in other words, the ones that are most likely to be important in determining an identification. For the remainder, the birdwatcher must refer to one of the far more detailed works of reference that are available.

Symbols and abbreviations

Where plumage variations have been illustrated, the following symbols have been used:

Imm. (Immature). This is taken to include all juvenile (i.e. the first full plumage after the downy stage) and transitional plumages until full adult plumage is attained.

   ♂   Male
   ♀   Female

Unless specifically labelled otherwise, illustrations are of birds in full adult plumage.

PARTS OF A BIRD

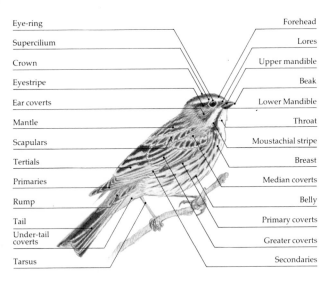

Eye-ring

Supercilium

Crown

Eyestripe

Ear coverts

Mantle

Scapulars

Tertials

Primaries

Rump

Tail

Under-tail coverts

Tarsus

Forehead

Lores

Upper mandible

Beak

Lower Mandible

Throat

Moustachial stripe

Breast

Median coverts

Belly

Primary coverts

Greater coverts

Secondaries

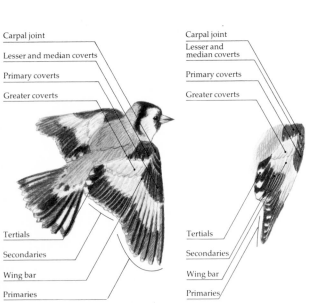

Carpal joint

Lesser and median coverts

Primary coverts

Greater coverts

Tertials

Secondaries

Wing bar

Primaries

Carpal joint

Lesser and median coverts

Primary coverts

Greater coverts

Tertials

Secondaries

Wing bar

Primaries

SKETCHING BIRDS
Philip Snow

This book is specifically designed to further an interest in sketching birds, or at least to encourage you to look a little harder at them and make notes wherever possible. Try to watch the bird as long as you can before attempting to draw it, and make as many plumage notes and other observations as the time allows. If you are really interested in learning to draw birds, the best places to begin are public park lakes, zoos, wildlife parks, farmyards and of course your own bird tables and gardens. This section is only intended as a basic introduction to bird sketching, and I advise those really interested to consult the books and articles that deal specifically with the subject, some of which are listed below. In addition, you can consult the many books and courses dealing with art instruction in general.

Although wildlife in collections are usually in unnatural surroundings, they offer splendid opportunities for relatively close and prolonged views, enabling you to study basic shape and activities such as resting, preening, feeding, stretching and so on. It soon becomes obvious that the larger birds which prefer more open habitats are prime models for study, both in collections and in the wild, and of these the herons and allies, swans, ducks and gulls are often the most approachable.

The greatest bird artists have always made use of the unfortunately frequent victims of accidents, and one can often find dead birds by the roadside, or after cold spells, and these are invaluable for furthering anatomical knowledge and 'feather mapping' – learning the groupings of feathers and how they fall into place on the bird whilst in flight or on the ground (how, for instance, the pale edged secondaries become a pale wing panel when folded with the bird at rest). Birds usually have the same numbers of feathers in the same groupings (see Parts of a Bird, opposite), but the shapes vary widely from one species to another.

Comparison of the wings of Song Thrush and Gannet (not to scale)

Today, in addition to the birds themselves, we have a rich selection of bird imagery to view, with the profusion of books (illustrated with photographs or paintings or both), television programmes and video all adding to our knowledge. They can all be of great help to the bird studier, *but there is no substitute for study from life*, as the sketchbooks and works of Charles Tunnicliffe, Lars Jonsson, Eric Ennion, and that sadly underexposed giant of wildlife portraiture, Bruno Liljefors, all show.

At the very simplest level, one can often start sketches with the basic shapes beloved of children's 'how to draw' books and build birds out of certain forms. The familiar tits and garden birds, especially when fluffed out in winter, can often be started from a circle with a few 'projecting' additions. But be warned: birds often change shape, even from one moment to the next, and an alert Heron is a very different shape to a relaxed Heron, and completely different again from the alert or relaxed Blue Tit.

The changing shapes of birds: Blue Tit in winter, relaxed and alert; Grey Heron relaxed and alert (note how the crest is raised and lowered).

The shape changes are caused by birds raising or lowering, relaxing or tightening, certain areas of feathers in response to excitement, mating ritual, feeding, preening, threat, heat or cold, and need continuous study if they are to be understood. It can be very frustrating to watch a bird move just as you were sketching it, and it is a good idea to leave that sketch unfinished, and start another one of a new pose, as the bird will often return to its former position. (But note that a flock of birds will often contain other individuals in a similar pose, which can be used for reference when finishing off the original sketch.)

An attempt to reduce a flock of Redshanks to simple outlines: note the different postures – (from left to right) relaxed, roosting, alert, feeding.

So far, we have been considering birds mainly as outlines, with the harder task of representing the three-dimensional form still to come. The form of the bird is obviously strongly influenced by its underlying skeleton, and the position of the legs and the beak must be seen to project from the correct places! This also frequently changes in the case of the legs, and many bird illustrators would probably admit that the legs and feet are the hardest part to depict.

The late Eric Ennion advised study of partly fledged nestlings as a good means of studying basic musculature and underlying bone (see *The Living Birds of Eric Ennion*, Gollancz, London 1982). His student, John Busby, points out (in his excellent three-part article 'How to Draw Birds' in the R.S.P.B. magazine *BIRDS*, 1984/5) that studying a plucked chicken carcase will show how the legs, which appear to depend from the deep chest muscles are in fact joined further back from the pelvis in a zig-zag arrangement.

Very basic skeletal diagrams of Greenshank and Mute Swan.

Birds in flight are normally harder to depict, but close study of wings (dead bird's wings are easy to dry and preserve in different positions) and wildlife films will help enormously. As with birds on the ground, the wings and tail frequently change shape, depending on whether the bird is gliding, soaring or flapping, and again it is the larger, slower birds that afford easiest models. It is best to begin with 'flat' studies, from above and below (here again, dead birds are very helpful) before tackling the more difficult perspectives.

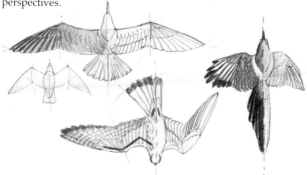

Simplified flight plans to show fan action of tail and wing feather layouts; top, gull soaring, tail fanned; left gull gliding, tail closed, wings angled back; above, Kestrel stooping; right, Magpie.

As usual, Charles Tunnicliffe provides an excellent model, and study of his published sketchbooks will show how, for instance, the leisurely flight of the Short-eared and Barn Owls can be depicted very effectively with a simple cylinder (for the body) and flat planes (for the wings). He then – as a master of foreshortening and perspective – builds on these shapes to give a vivid, life-like representation of the bird (for unless a bird is directly above or below us, the two wings will be different shapes.

Basic studies of form and foreshortening: top, Shelducks in fast direct flight; below, gulls soaring and gliding.

Most of the finest portraits of birds are executed with the minimum of lines or brushstrokes, loosely and fluidly suggesting movement and alertness (see especially *A Sketchbook of Birds*, Gollancz, London 1979, *Sketches of Birdlife*, Gollancz 1981, and 'Bird Portraiture', the *Studio* 1945, all by Charles Tunnicliffe). Camera and film technology has provided us with ultra-detailed close-ups of birds, but field views are generally of a briefer and more distant nature, where individual feather detail is lost to an overall view of feather groupings. Raymond Ching commented that too much detail in a bird painting helps to 'stop' that bird (*Studies and Sketches of a Bird Painter*, Landsdowne, Melbourne 1980), a statement endorsed by Gunnar Brusewitz (*Wings and Seasons*, Croom Helm, London 1980), in a discussion of how split second photography can freeze the otherwise fluid motion of a bird into isolated and awkward positions, normally too fleeting for the eye to see. We have to select our own lines out of the mass of information provided and hope to depict birds' usually graceful movements in a like manner.

As noted earlier, this can only be an introduction to a very complex and pleasurable pursuit, which, strictly speaking, needs continuous application. But this should not mar the pleasure nor turn birdwatching into a hard chore. Do not be afraid of making mistakes nor of leaving lots of unfinished drawings, as this is really the only way to learn. I think that it was the great Victorian bird artist, Joseph Wolf, who said that we only draw well that which we know thoroughly, and you might find yourself learning an awful lot about birds when you really start to observe and note. I certainly did.

SOCIETIES TO JOIN

As your interest develops, you will probably soon recognise the benefits of joining a local or national society, or both. Not only does this bring you into contact with others with the same interest, but it will bring the opportunity of organised outings, regular publications, newsletters and indoor meetings and lectures. Local bird clubs cover most parts of the country (details are available from the local public library). The R.S.P.B., the largest ornithological organisation in Britain, offers members access to its network of bird reserves as well as a high-quality quarterly magazine (details from The Royal Society for the Protection of Birds, The Lodge, Sandy, Bedfordshire). For anyone who would like to make a genuine contribution to the study of birds and bird life in Britain by taking part in more structured field work – regular censuses, special surveys – the British Trust for Ornithology (Beech Grove, Tring, Hertfordshire) offers opportunities on a country-wide scale.

THE BIRDWATCHER'S CODE OF CONDUCT

At all times, remember to observe the following code:

1. The welfare of birds must come first.
2. Habitat must be protected.
3. Keep disturbance to birds and their habitats to a minimum.
4. When you find a rare bird think carefully about whom you should tell.
5. Do not harass rare migrants.
6. Abide by the Bird Protection Acts at all times.
7. Respect the rights of landowners.
8. Respect the rights of other people in the countryside.
9. Make your records available to the local bird recorder.
10. Behave abroad as you would when birdwatching at home.

Great Northern Diver (above): note
pale area around eye – absent in Black-
throated – and different head-shape.

Compare head and bill with rare **White-
billed Diver** (top).

Imm.

Black-throated Div

Transitional

Note up-tilted head and bill of **Red-
throated Diver** (above). Divers search
for prey with head submerged (below).

Black-throated Diver (above) has a
lighter bill which thereby appears to be
longer and straighter.

Dabchick (above): easily identified by
minute, compact form and active
behaviour. Often on inland waters.

*Black-
necked*

Slavoni

Black-necked Grebe (above) is difficult
to distinguish from **Slavonian Grebe**
(right). See text opposite.

The **Great Crested Grebe** (below) is
more slender-necked than Red-necked,
with whiter face and breast.

Note **Red-necked Grebe's** (below)
stockier form than Great Crested and
duskier face and breast.

Imm.

Great Crested

Red-necked

DIVERS AND GREBES: WINTER

Divers and grebes often frequent the same inshore waters in winter. They fly very little and are usually seen on the water. All species adopt similar winter plumage patterns – dark above and white below. Separating the two groups is the first essential; also beware distant Cormorants and Merganser (see silhouettes below). Divers are bulky, tailless, low in the water, and sleek-headed with large spear-shaped bills. Grebes are smaller and slimmer and have more angular heads and an alert, upright posture.

The **Great Northern Diver** and **Black-throated Diver** are particularly difficult to separate, especially as only one species is usually present and there is no opportunity for comparison. Black-throated Divers show a white patch towards the rear of the body just above the water line, but it can be difficult to see on choppy water at a distance. They have a low sloping forehead compared to the Great Northern's slightly angular one. The Black-throated's upperparts are uniformly dusky black (but immatures look 'scaly' in good light) whereas Great Northern's show secondary barring. The Great Northern is a large bulky bird with a shortish thick neck and very substantial bill; remnants of the breeding pattern (see next page) are often retained into early winter. A dark semi-collar shows at the base of the neck. Because it is less deep, the Black-throated Diver's bill appears longer and straighter, but such differences are difficult to see at long range.

The most helpful character for identifying the **Red-throated Diver** at a distance is the marked upward tilt of the head and bill. Otherwise it is altogether a slenderer and paler bird than the other two, with a finer bill. The back is flecked white all over (immatures browner and less flecked). The dark of crown and nape merges with the white of throat and neck without producing a sharp line.

Of the smaller grebes, the **Dabchick** or **Little Grebe** presents fewest problems. The smallest of our true water birds (10"/25cm), it is almost exaggeratedly blunt-ended. It often seems to spend its entire winter diving repeatedly!. It occurs more often inland than other grebes (except Great Crested) in winter.

Slavonian and **Black-necked Grebes** are notoriously tricky to separate. Markedly larger than Dabchick, both are much smaller than Great Crested. The Black-necked Grebe has a fairly short neck and a fine up-tilted bill; also the dark crown comes lower down the cheek and merges indefinitely with the white, whereas in the Slavonian there is a 'cleaner' separation between the two at eye level; the resulting whitish collar on the Slavonian is much more obvious from the back than it is in the Black-necked.

Great Crested Grebes and **Red-necked Grebes** are similar-looking birds in winter, often difficult to separate at a distance. Both occur on inshore waters but only the Great Crested normally uses freshwater lakes. The larger Great Crested is white-headed and has a clean distinction between the dark upperparts and white underside, whereas the Red-necked Grebe is duskier, with a different head pattern, and lacks the 'ears'. The Red-necked Grebe's bill has a yellow base.

Below: winter silhouettes. From left to right; Red-throated Diver, Cormorant, Merganser, Grebe.

Black-throated Diver (above) breeds on larger freshwater lochs than Red-throated.

Red-throated Diver.

The **Red-throated Diver** (left) is the slimmest and (slightly) the smallest of the three British divers.

A few **Great Northern Divers** (below) summer offshore in Scotland but do not breed and are accidental inland at any season.

Great Crested Grebe has unique head decorations (above) and elaborate breeding season display

Both **Black-necked** and **Slavonian Grebe** (bottom) have distinctive sprays of golden head feathers, forming 'horns' in the case of the Slavonian, which also lacks the black neck.

Great Crested

The yellow gape at the base of the **Dabchick's** bill (below) produces an obvious pale facial spot at a distance. From the rear, it has a surprisingly wide profile.

Slavonian

Black necke

DIVERS AND GREBES: SUMMER

Only two species of breeding divers or grebes – Great Crested Grebe and Dabchick – regularly nest in England or Wales. All others, with the exception of the Red-necked Grebe, breed with different degrees of scarcity or rarity in Scotland. Sexes are alike in all species.

The **Red-throated Diver** is a scarce breeding bird in W. and N. Scotland: 700-800 pairs breed, widely scattered on small lochans with fringes of cotton grass and other vegetation on remote moorlands. Most of these breeding lochs are too small to feed on and so birds regularly fly back and forth to sea lochs for food. The dull vineous-red throat is usually seen only as a dark patch except at close quarters or in extremely good light. Like other divers, it is entirely aquatic and aerial, coming to land only to nest and then only a few feet from the water's edge. When preening on the water, birds roll onto their sides and present the white underparts conspicuously. They often raise themselves in the water to flap their wings.

The **Black-throated Diver** is a rarer breeding bird, no more than 100 pairs or so breeding in much the same areas as the Red-throated Diver, but typically on much larger lochs. In summer, the pale grey head removes any risk of confusion with the **Great Northern Diver** (which is rare in the breeding season anyway). The chequered pattern on the upperparts separates both from the Red-throated Diver.

The **Great Crested Grebe** is an unmistakable bird in the breeding season when it is adorned with colourful neck ruff and tippets. It breeds on large or moderately large water bodies especially in the lowlands and is widespread. It seldom flies. In spring, watch for the elaborate courtship displays, involving much posturing and exaggerated use of the head and neck decorations.

Great Crested Grebe: courtship display

The **Black-necked Grebe** and **Slavonian Grebe** are strikingly coloured birds in summer. Both are very rare breeders, mainly in Scotland – the Black-necked exclusively so.

The **Dabchick or Little Grebe** is a widely distributed and common breeding bird, mainly on lowland waters, although it does not necessarily shun upland pools providing that they have reasonable vegetation cover; it happily occupies small pools as well as large. The Dabchick has a distinctive call, most aptly described as a whinnying trill, lasting about four seconds. The Dabchick's size and shape should preclude confusion with any other species.

Grey Herons

Imm.

Purple Heron

The **Grey Heron** is grey bodied with a black and white head, heavy dagger bill and slender black crest. Immatures are more uniformly grey and lack the adult's long black plumes. In flight, the Heron's bowed-wing silhouette is unmistakable.

In flight the folded neck of **Purple Heron** produces a more bulging shape than in Grey Heron. Slender neck with thin black lines on chestnut background (right) is distinctive.

Bittern

The **Night Heron** (above) spends much time perched in trees: active at dusk.

The tiny **Little Bittern** (below) may occur in a wide range of wetland habitats. It climbs easily among the reeds.

Bitterns (below) are tawny coloured with dark barring. They fly languidly over the reed-bed, legs trailing (above).

HERONS, BITTERNS, CRANE

The familiar **Grey Heron** is a ubiquitous wetland bird. Sexes are alike. It typically hunts shallow waters, standing statuesque and motionless and making a lightning stab at passing prey. It also stalks through marsh vegetation looking for frogs, large insects, and small mammals. Much of the most intensive feeding is done at first light. In flight, the silhouette is unmistakable (but see Purple Heron): it has very deep, slow wing beats with neck withdrawn and legs extended behind. Often adopts a single-leg stance at rest.

The **Purple Heron** occurs patchily in western Europe as far north as Holland, where it is still increasing. In Britain, it is a rare but regular visitor, usually in spring (but some stay longer) and mainly in eastern and southern counties. It is exclusively a reed-bed bird, more secretive and furtive than the Grey Heron: also less bulky and darker plumaged with a more serpentine appearance. In flight the Purple Heron is less laboured, with narrower wings (which show a reddish-brown panel underneath), a more obviously coiled neck and disproportionately large feet. On the ground, the sandy-coloured immatures could be confused with Grey Heron but differences of size, shape and form are sufficient to distinguish them quickly. Immatures take two years to adopt full adult plumage.

Bitterns are reed-bed birds, very secretive and shy, which keep well out of view most of the time and can be very difficult to see. The tawny-plumaged Bittern is beautifully cryptically coloured, especially when hiding, with elongated neck and pointed bill. Birds feed mainly within the reed-bed but can sometimes be seen on the reed-edge, especially at dawn and dusk. They move with a hunched gait and lowered head. As they are so elusive, their presence is most easily detected in the breeding season by the strange far-carrying call of the male, a resonant 'booming' like the sound of a distant foghorn, and a characteristic sound of the reed-beds in which they breed. They are now sadly rare in Britain, mainly found in East Anglia and a few reed-beds in the west.

The rare **Little Bittern** is only half the size of the Bittern and much more strongly patterned. Sexes are similarly patterned but male's upperparts are markedly darker and the female's streakier. In flight, the pale wing coverts contrast strongly with remaining dark areas of the wings. Young birds are tawny with very heavy streaking. A few Little Bitterns occur from late March to September in most years; they occupy a wider spectrum of wetland habitats than the Bittern and are extremely skulking. They fly with rapid wing-beats alternating with short glides.

Also rare is the **Night Heron**, which breeds northwards as far as Holland and occurs occasionally in eastern England, although a feral colony has established in Edinburgh. Adults are unmistakable. Immatures are much more like the Bittern.

The **Crane** is a huge long-legged, long-necked bird, occurring annually in small but increasing numbers. It is distinctive in flight with its long neck extended straight (see silhouette below). It has black and grey plumage and a prominent white cheek stripe.

Cranes in flight

21

WHITE EGRETS AND ALLIES

Non-breeding

Breeding

Spoonbills

White Stork

Cattle Egret

The vagrant **Cattle Egret** is more
hunched, stockier and less hyper-active
than Little Egret. Usually feeds in drier
areas, often amongst stock. The
dazzling **Little Egret** has slender head
and neck, black rapier bill and bright
yellow feet. It feeds in shallow water,
chasing fast with darting bill.

Spoonbills (top) feed in shallow pools;
they have strange spatulate bills and, in
the breeding season, buff breast bands
and ragged crests. Increasingly seen in
E. England (May-Oct.). **White Storks**
(above) may 'overshoot' from Europe.

*Breeding
Plumes*

*Little
Egrets*

Non-breeding

Egrets fly with necks withdrawn: *Spoonbill and Stork with necks extended.*

Mute

Whooper

Bewick's

Mute Swans

Imm. 1st year

Imm. 2nd year

Bill patterns and colours distinguish swan species at all ages; note particularly the Mute Swan's black knob and the difference in pattern of yellow on Bewick's and Whooper. Juvenile swans pose few problems as they are always with parents.

The familiar **Mute Swan** (above) is resident on inland waters and estuaries. **Whooper** and **Bewick's Swans** (below) are winter visitors only. Sexes are alike. Whoopers often produce loud trumpeting, especially in flight; Mutes are silent; Bewick's have an excitable nasal cackling.

Bewick's

Whooper

Mute

The Mute Swan's curved-neck posture identifies it from the other two which normally stand or swim with straight necks.

Mute Swan (left) flies with rhythmic soughing of wings; Whooper (centre) and Bewick's with silent wings.

Greylags

The **Greylag** is a large, pale, thickset goose with orange bill and pink legs; there is an obvious similarity in shape and form with the farmyard goose which derives from it.

Pinkfoot

Bean Goose

Bean Geese: elongated head-and-bill shape; variable orange band on bill.

Pinkfoot

The **Pinkfoot** has a short neck, small, neat head and noticeable contrast between grey body and dark head and neck (far left, in flight). Legs and feet pink. Note short black-and-pink bill.

Whitefronts

Whitefronts are identified by the white patch at base of bill and black bars on breast. Immatures lack both features. European Whitefronts have pink bills but the Greenland birds are generally darker and have orange bills.

Greenland race

European race

Imm.

Lesser Whitefront

'Grey' geese are winter visitors in large numbers, especially to Scotland.

Small numbers of wild **Greylag Geese** breed in N. and W. Scotland and a few feral populations have established elsewhere. Other than these, large flocks of Greylags from Iceland winter in Scotland from October to mid-April, feeding on stubble in autumn and moving to grassland in spring. The Greylag is a heavy-looking goose with a large prominent head and thick-set neck, both features evident on the ground and in flight. It has a substantial orange bill and pink legs and is the easiest of the grey geese to distinguish in flight because of its heavy-headed appearance and the particularly striking pale forewing. Identification is also much aided by the familiar 'farmyard goose' call, two- or three-syllabled: *"aahng, aahng, aahng"*.

The entire Iceland and Greenland population of **Pink-footed Geese** winters in Scotland and northern England, arriving in September and feeding in large flocks on stubble and root fields. In flight the short-necked, small-headed silhouette is important; the flocks, almost always in Vs, fly faster and with quicker wing beats than other grey geese; also note the contrast of the pale forewing, although not as obvious as in the Greylag. Pinkfeet are noisier than other grey geese with a higher pitched call, a repeated *"wink wink"*.

Bean Geese are larger than Pinkfeet – almost as large as Greylag – and, like them have dark heads and necks, although the head shape is very different. Very few Bean Geese reach Britain each year: there are usually only two regular flocks, one in the Yare valley in Norfolk, the other near the River Ken in S.W. Scotland, arriving in the New Year and leaving again by the end of March. In severe winters, other small flocks occur in S.E. England, otherwise odd individuals occasionally appear in flocks of other Siberian species (usually Whitefronts). Bean Geese are uniformly dark brown birds and in flight the fairly long, thin neck and elongated head and bill are useful characters. The bill has a black base and tip with a variable band of orange between. Legs are normally bright orange. Bean Geese are generally silent.

Two separate populations of **White-fronted Geese** winter in Britain: birds of the Greenland race winter in Ireland and W. Scotland (where they often associate with Greylags) with one flock in Wales, while birds of the Siberian race, which winter mainly in the Low Countries, occur in sizeable flocks at Slimbridge, Glos., in the Avon Valley, Hants, and at a few other sites. Greenland birds are noticeably darker than Siberian, and feed largely on acid boglands. In flight, both have an all-over grey-brown appearance and are longer necked than Pinkfeet. They are quite noisy and the somewhat laughing musical call is a variable *"kiao-kiock"*.

Individuals of the rare **Lesser White-fronted Goose** occasionally turn up with flocks of other goose species from Arctic Europe. It is a distinctly smaller and neater goose than the European Whitefront and the facial patch is a different shape. Note too the short stubby bill and the distinguishing yellow eye-ring at closer range. An individual amongst a flock of another species can often be located by its quicker movements and faster feeding.

Canada Geese

The long black neck of the **Canada Goose** (above) contrasts strongly with the brown body and white cheek patch.

The smaller black-and-white **Barnacle Goose** (below and left) is a winter visitor to Scotland and Ireland.

Barnacle Geese

Brent Geese (below) are small and dark with short necks and a narrow white necklace (not on immatures). Siberian (dark-bellied) are distinct from Greenland (pale-bellied) birds.

Brent Geese

With red bill, bottle-green head and neck and broad chestnut chest band, **Shelducks** are unmistakable 'black-and-white' birds. Pairs defend feeding territories on the mudflats, not the nest site itself. Male has prominent knob at base of bill.

♀

Shelducks

♂

imm.

'BLACK GEESE', SHELDUCK
EGYPTIAN GOOSE

The **Canada Goose** is the largest of all our geese. An introduced species, it is increasing in numbers rapidly in town parks and other urban areas as well as on rural waters. It is principally an inland species, unlike the other two 'black' geese. Canada Geese are highly gregarious, flocks often numbering several hundreds. They feed mainly by grazing on cropped grasslands and walk easily and well on land. They also head-dip and up-end in water to take aquatic plants. Individual ganders can be very aggressive to human and other intruders near the nest site. Flocks fly in deep chevrons or long lines.

The **Barnacle Goose**, much smaller than the Canada Goose, winters in Ireland and W. Scotland from populations in Iceland, Greenland and Svalbard; Islay, in the Inner Hebrides (20,000+) is the principal site. Occasional individuals (including escaped birds from collections) may turn up almost anywhere from time to time. Black and white plumage and white face make the bird unmistakable. Flocks on the wing produce a continuous dog-like yapping. They feed on coastal pastures and usually resort to sea lochs and inlets at night.

Only a little larger than Mallard, the dusky little **Brent Geese** feed on mudflats (e.g. Thames estuary, N. Norfolk coast, Lincolnshire, river Exe) and, more recently, in coastal fields of winter cereals and pasture. Although reasonably easy to identify on the ground or water, Brent Geese can be confused with large duck (e.g. Mallard) or possibly even Barnacle Geese when on the wing, especially when the winter light is poor. In flight, they are all-dark except for the distinctive white patch at the rear end. They usually fly in straggling lines and flocks produce a distinctive nasal grumbling noise; the main call is a two-note *"wok, wok"*. On coastal fields, the birds keep in tight flocks, moving quickly over the ground. When swimming, they sit high in the water with tails cocked and heads leaning forward, giving a distinctive silhouette. Two races occur in winter: pale-bellied birds from Greenland (wintering in Ireland) and Svalbard (wintering on Lindisfarne) and the dark-bellied Siberian birds, wintering in S. and E. England.

The boldly coloured, rather goose-like, **Shelduck** is primarily a bird of mudflats and low coastlines, occurring only sparingly inland. Sexes are similar, but the male has a prominent knob at the base of its red bill. The only fleeting confusion possible may be with the drake Shoveler (see pp. 28-29) when swimming, but Shoveler do not use salt water. Like many ducks, the sexes have distinct calls, although seldom used outside the breeding season. The female has a loud nasal *"aak, aak, aak…"* (produced occasionally by the drake) and the drake has a soft sibilant *"whee-ooo"*. Both in flight and at a distance, Shelducks are unlikely to offer any real problem of identification, and although immatures are rather nondescript they are almost invariably in the company of adults.

The somewhat unusual **Egyptian Goose** (below) relates more to the Shelducks than to true geese. In flight it shows white forewings, black primaries and green secondaries. There are small feral populations in Norfolk and one or two other sites in southern England.

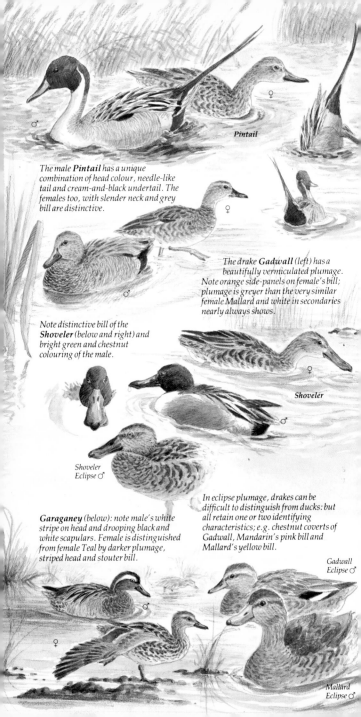

Pintail

The male **Pintail** has a unique combination of head colour, needle-like tail and cream-and-black undertail. The females too, with slender neck and grey bill are distinctive.

The drake **Gadwall** (left) has a beautifully vermiculated plumage. Note orange side-panels on female's bill; plumage is greyer than the very similar female Mallard and white in secondaries nearly always shows.

Note distinctive bill of the **Shoveler** (below and right) and bright green and chestnut colouring of the male.

Shoveler

Shoveler Eclipse ♂

Garaganey (below): note male's white stripe on head and drooping black and white scapulars. Female is distinguished from female Teal by darker plumage, striped head and stouter bill.

In eclipse plumage, drakes can be difficult to distinguish from ducks: but all retain one or two identifying characteristics; e.g. chestnut coverts of Gadwall, Mandarin's pink bill and Mallard's yellow bill.

Gadwall Eclipse ♂

Mallard Eclipse ♂

DUCKS: DABBLING DUCKS
MAINLY FEEDING ON WATER

Ducks pose a variety of identification problems because, although the drakes are usually distinctive, many of the females have very similar cryptic colouring. Added to this, all wildfowl undergo a full moult in late summer which, for the males, involves a much drabber plumage phase – the eclipse plumage (see opposite) At this stage even such familiar birds as Mallard drakes become so similar to the females that they can be separated only with care.

DABBLING DUCKS: FRESHWATER. The species illustrated on this page normally feed only on water.

The **Pintail** is a graceful, long-necked duck, flighty and fairly nervous. It is a surface feeder, upending in deepish water (30cm/1ft) using its long neck to reach the bottom. It swims fairly high, usually with neck erect and tail raised. The male's long pointed tail is distinctive; the only other duck with a similar tail is the Long-tailed Duck (pp. 34-35) which is principally marine. Pintail nest very sparingly in Britain in widely scattered localities; they are much more numerous in winter with particularly big flocks on the Mersey and Dee estuaries.

The **Gadwall** is a somewhat retiring and inconspicuous duck, preferring reedy pools with plenty of cover. It feeds in much the same way as the larger Mallard and often in company with it. Both sexes have a distinctive white patch on the wing in flight, when the male's chestnut secondary coverts are also revealed. The male's black under-tail and dark bill also aid identification. On the water Gadwall swim fairly high and tend to hold their tails higher than Mallard (rather like Teal). It is most numerous in East Anglia where the breeding pairs probably originated from feral stock; in Scotland (especially Loch Leven) and Ireland the small breeding populations are probably of genuinely wild origin: elsewhere it is mainly a local winter visitor. Gadwall tend to be seen more in pairs through the year than other ducks.

The **Shoveler** is easily distinguished from all other duck species by its large spatulate bill which is as easily seen when the bird is on the wing as when it is on water. It feeds sitting low on the water and dabbling with head outstretched, or submerged; it does not upend as regularly as other species, but when it does its orange feet are usually conspicuous. In flight the relatively long neck gives the wings the appearance of being set far back. It is a thinly distributed breeding species and winter visitor.

The only duck which is exclusively a summer visitor, breeding sparingly in lowland England, is the little **Garganey**, closely related to the Teal. It is amongst the earliest arrivals, from early March on. The only likely confusion can be with the similar-sized Teal, but the conspicuous white stripe on the male's head separates them easily; at a distance it appears as a rich brown duck with bright white supercilium. The male can also be distinguished by the sharp line between dark breast and pale underparts which is also visible in flight. It is a rather unobtrusive duck prefering shallow lowland pools with plenty of cover. Despite the small bill, it resembles the Shoveler rather than the Teal in its feeding habits. Birds usually occur as isolated individuals, pairs or small parties, not in flocks.

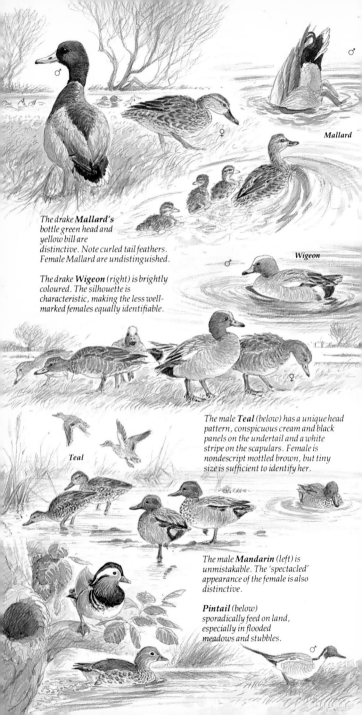

*The drake **Mallard's** bottle green head and yellow bill are distinctive. Note curled tail feathers. Female Mallard are undistinguished.*

*The drake **Wigeon** (right) is brightly coloured. The silhouette is characteristic, making the less well-marked females equally identifiable.*

*The male **Teal** (below) has a unique head pattern, conspicuous cream and black panels on the undertail and a white stripe on the scapulars. Female is nondescript mottled brown, but tiny size is sufficient to identify her.*

*The male **Mandarin** (left) is unmistakable. The 'spectacled' appearance of the female is also distinctive.*

***Pintail** (below) sporadically feed on land, especially in flooded meadows and stubbles.*

Mallard

Wigeon

Teal

DABBLING DUCKS: FRESHWATER REGULARLY FEEDING ON LAND

The species illustrated on this page all regularly feed on land as well as water.

The **Mallard** or 'wild duck' is by far the most numerous of our wildfowl and the most familiar. In addition to wild populations – which include birds from Russia in winter – many are reared and released by wildfowlers. Mallard occupy a wide range of habitats, from ponds and lakes to rivers, ditches and marshes. Some birds use coastal waters. It is a largish, heavy duck which walks well on land and is a strong flier. On water Mallard feed either by surface sieving, or submerging the head or upending. On land they graze, goose-fashion. The drake's purple speculum, bordered black and white, is diagnostic. It is the only duck with curled tail feathers. The female is rather nondescript and similar to several other dabbling duck females. Only the female quacks.

Wigeon are numerous winter visitors (but a few hundred pairs also breed, mainly in Scotland) to coastal marshes and inland flood meadows. They are the most terrestrial of our duck species. Grazing flocks, or birds roosting on water, are easily located by the clear whistling *"whee-ooo"* of the males. Females have a more rufous plumage than other female dabbling ducks and are short-billed. No other duck species grazes in dense packs as Wigeon do. Flocks sometimes feed on eel grass in muddy estuaries, often alongside Brent Geese. In upright stance Wigeon appear to have very short legs.

The **Teal** is our smallest duck and size alone usually identifies it (but see also Garganey pp. 28-29). Teal breed widely and occur in considerable numbers in winter on coastal marshes, inland waters and flooded fields. On water they feed by upending or by submerging their heads and sieving for seeds. They operate similarly in floodwater, walking slowly forward, sieving as they go; in rough wet grassland or marsh, many birds may be concealed at any one time. They are fairly vocal and the male has a very characteristic *"kritt"* call; females have a harsh, high pitched quack. As early as January birds may be paired up in the winter flocks. both sexes have a green speculum and accompanying white wing bar.

The improbably beautiful **Mandarin** is a species introduced from eastern China and now slowly spreading in the wild in Britain, especially S.E. England and the Cheshire area. The male is completely unmistakable and the 'spectacled' appearance of the greyish female is reasonably distinctive too; her pale brownish breast and flanks are heavily marked with rows of whitish spots. They occur on wooded freshwaters – lakes, meres, slow-moving rivers and ornamental ponds. Mandarins feed both on land and in the water, usually in association with trees which provide both food (acorns etc.) and hole nesting sites. Pairs take readily to nesting boxes.

Several feral species or variants may also be encountered, including the domesticated Aylesbury and crosses between this and Mallard (below left), and the ungainly Muscovy (below right).

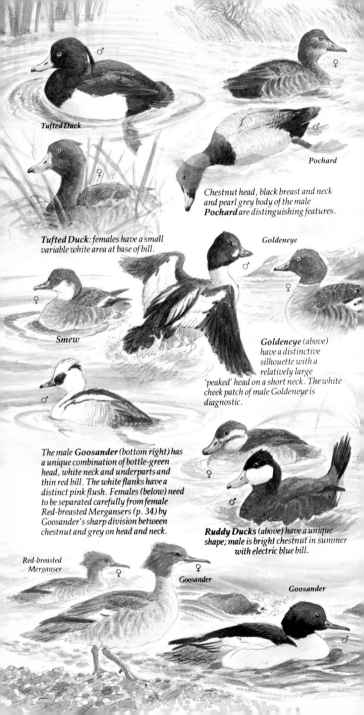

Tufted Duck

Pochard

Chestnut head, black breast and neck and pearl grey body of the male **Pochard** are distinguishing features.

Tufted Duck: females have a small variable white area at base of bill.

Goldeneye

Smew

Goldeneye (above) have a distinctive silhouette with a relatively large 'peaked' head on a short neck. The white cheek patch of male Goldeneye is diagnostic.

The male **Goosander** (bottom right) has a unique combination of bottle-green head, white neck and underparts and thin red bill. The white flanks have a distinct pink flush. Females (below) need to be separated carefully from female Red-breasted Mergansers (p. 34) by Goosander's sharp division between chestnut and grey on head and neck.

Ruddy Ducks (above) have a unique shape; male is bright chestnut in summer with electric blue bill.

Red-breasted Merganser

Goosander

Goosander

FRESHWATER DIVING DUCKS

The **Tufted Duck**, commonest of freshwater diving ducks, is a widespread bird on open waters - gravel pits, lakes, even urban waters. The male is a black duck with drooping crest (not easily visible at a distance), white flank panel and a bright yellow eye. The most likely plumage confusion is with the marine Scaup (pp. 34-35) but the two do not normally overlap in habitat requirements. Tufted Duck usually occur in smallish parties.

The **Pochard** is a common freshwater diving duck, often found in company with Tufted Ducks. Even in silhouette the Pochard is easily recognisable with its high crown and sloping forehead. The male is the only common duck with chestnut head and black bill with pale blue band. The rare Red-crested Pochard has a pink bill. The female, although dun-coloured, has the same head profile as the male, a brown head and foreparts and pale ring round the dark bill. Pochard are expert and active divers.

The **Goldeneye** uses both coastal and inland waters in winter. Small numbers breed in the Highlands of Scotland by freshwater lochs, but most others are winter visitors from N. Europe. The male has a distinctive piebald plumage but most birds are 'brown-heads' – females or immatures. The females have a white neck collar, lacking in immatures; both have chocolate brown heads with brilliant yellow eyes, and show a white patch on the closed wing. They usually occur individually or in small loose groups.

The elegant **Goosander** is a bird of clear waters, breeding in hollow trees on upland rivers, lakes and reservoirs and extending to lowland waters in winter. The Goosander is a large, longish and fairly heavily-built bird. The male is easily identified by colour and pattern and the silhouette, which shows a long, low body profile on the water, with prominent head and long thin bill. The red-headed females (and immatures) show a slight crest, greyish upperparts and a clear white throat and collar. The female's white chin, and the sharp division between chestnut head and white collar, separate it with certainty from the very similar female Red-breasted Merganser (see pp. 34-35). On winter waters there may be a slight risk of initial confusion of either sex with Goldeneye at a distance. Goosanders are timid birds and take flight readily.

Smews breed in the far N. of Finland and Russia and small numbers occur on large waters in southern England as winter visitors. They are 'saw-billed' ducks – like Merganser and Goosander – but much smaller than the others, only a little larger than a Teal. It is a very distinctive duck; the male has particularly beautiful plumage but the female also is easily identified.

The **Ruddy Duck**, a native of North America, has become naturalised in several counties in England and Wales. The male, with bright blue bill, chestnut body (summer only), black cap and nape contrasting with white cheeks, is uniquely coloured. In winter the male loses the chestnut and becomes grey-bodied. The female is similarly patterned to the winter male but has a dark stripe across her duskier white cheek. The slightly ludicrous 'stiff-tail' is the clinching identification feature. Confusion is possible between female or immature Smew and female Ruddy Duck.

Scaup (above) resemble Tufted Duck.
but are exclusively marine. Note
female's white facial patch.

Eiders

Scoters

The male **Eider** (above) has a diagnostic
shape and colour pattern. The
cryptically-coloured female is often
found on the shoreline with ducklings.

Imm. ♂

The dark brown female **Common Scoter**
(above) can look almost as black as the
male at a distance, but pale cheeks and
throat are reasonably visible.

Winter ♂

Summer ♂

Long-tailed Duck: winter
male is almost wholly white with dark
breast band, dark facial patch and long
tail. Summer plumage is entirely
different with complex transitional
phases.

Immature **Goldeneye** (below):
see p.32

Most female **Velvet Scoters** (above)
show two pale face patches. Note white
wing patch and heavier bill than
Common Scoter on both sexes.

The **Red-breasted Merganser** (below)
is found mainly on inshore waters and
estuaries, and is only likely to be
confused with Goosander (p. 32), which
is a freshwater duck.

All sea duck are diving ducks. The species illustrated here are normally saltwater birds, seldom occurring inland (except **Golden-eye** which is equally at home on either fresh or salt water: see pp. 32-33 for full description).

The **Scaup** is a winter visitor to British coasts and estuaries, with biggest numbers off the E. coast of Scotland. The male's pale grey back and the female's extensive white face patch distinguish both from the Tufted Duck – but note that female Tufted Duck often has a small white mark round the base of the bill. They usually occur in large flocks rather than small groups. At a distance the males look dark at either end and white in between. Birds sometimes use freshwater pools close to the shore, especially in severe weather.

Eiders are resident ducks which breed numerously round northern coasts from the Farne Islands on the E. to Cumbria and N. Ireland on the W. coast. They are large, heavy looking birds, long-headed and rather short-necked. The males are uniquely patterned and coloured although at sea they may appear essentially white above and black below. Exclusively marine, they live close inshore and are highly gregarious. The combination of brightly coloured males and dun females is easily identifiable, even at a considerable distance. Young males go through several stages of piebald transitional plumage before attaining full adult plumage.

The male **Common Scoter** is our only wholly black duck. Usually strictly marine, flocks are often large. They are frequently well out from the shoreline. Small numbers breed on moorland in N.W. Britain and N. Ireland, but otherwise it occurs offshore in favoured (sandy-bottomed) areas throughout the year, being especially numerous in winter.

The rarer **Velvet Scoter** is similarly marine, being even more at home in rough waters. It is a winter visitor, mainly to the eastern seaboard south to Kent, with largest concentrations off N.E. Scotland. It is more likely to be seen closer inshore than the Common Scoter which is the only species with which confusion is likely to arise (but beware of Black Guillemot, pp.74-75). Both sexes show the vivid white wing patch which distinguishes them from the slightly smaller Common Scoter. It has a proportionately larger head than Common Scoter and a yellower bill.

The beautiful **Long-tailed Duck** is unmistakable at any time of the year. Winter visitors to northern and eastern coasts, they are essentially marine and often well offshore, although odd individuals use coastal pools, inland reservoirs etc. The female lacks the male's long tail; her white head always has a dark crown but the pattern of the head patches varies through the autumn and winter. Uniquely amongst our ducks it has an entirely different breeding plumage (rarely seen in Britain).

The **Red-breasted Merganser** is a longish slender duck with long fine red bill and a ragged crest. It inhabits estuaries, sheltered bays and sea lochs, mainly on the western side of Britain north from Cardigan Bay but also occurs on rivers and lakes. Large gatherings of young birds are regular in estuaries in late summer. The male is distinctive with bottle-green head, white collar and brown (not red) breast flecked with black.

DUCKS IN FLIGHT

Common Scoter

Velvet Scoter

Eider: *heavy looking, flight very low over sea.*

Common Scoter: *usually seen as distant line of all-black ducks low over sea.* **Velvet Scoter** *show white wing panels on jet black plumage: sometimes with Common Scoter.*

Scaup *(above): beware similarity with Tufted Duck*

Long-tailed Duck *(winter): wing beats are deep, well below body level, unlike any other duck: characteristic flight, swinging from side to side.*

Goldeneye *(right): white wing patch extends almost to front of wing. Very fast flight and whistling wings.*

Red-breasted Merganser *(above): slender silhouette: low over water.* **Pintail** *(below) high-flying and very fast: long neck and pointed tail.*

Pintail

♀ *Mallard*

Mallard: *purple speculum bordered by white bars: fast flight*

Wigeon: males have white wing patch and white V in tail.

Teal (above): fast, erratic flight in compact parties; almost vertical take-off.

Tufted Duck (above) from below are black either end and white in between: **Pochard** (right) is similar but lacks broad white bar on upper wing.

Pochard

Gadwall

Garganey (above): Teal-sized with prominent pale blue forewing on male. **Shoveler** (right): the large spatulate bill is prominent in flight.

Gadwall (above): white wing patch on inner secondaries is distinguishing feature.

Goosander (below): male appears white with dark head and prominent wing patches. Heavier-bodied than Merganser.

'Ringtails'

Hen Harriers

♀ ♂

The male **Hen Harrier** is so pale as to
appear almost gull-like. Note dark
trailing edge to wings and lack of black
line on secondaries. Female and first
winter birds are similar (but immature
males are smaller).

♂

Montagu's
Harriers

♀

Black wing bars and 'smoky' grey rump
patch, together with even lighter flight
distinguish the male **Montagu's
Harrier** from Hen Harrier.

♂ ♀

The **Marsh Harrier**
is a summer visitor,
and exclusively a reed-
bed bird.

BIRDS OF PREY: HARRIERS

Birds of prey can be extremely difficult to identify, and inexperienced birdwatchers may often have to leave a problem of identification unresolved. Most sightings are of birds in flight, often at a distance and with little showing by way of colours or pattern. Conventional illustrations indicating species perched and in full colour are far removed from reality in the field – only the Buzzard and Kestrel are regularly likely to be seen perched. In flight, it is important to look at – and to make notes and, if possible, accurate sketches of – the basic shape, type of flight, tail and wing proportions and flight profile; remember too the areas and seasons in which you are most likely to see different species. Females are larger than males in all species.

Three harrier species occur in Britain (only one, the Hen Harrier, in Ireland). They are light-bodied birds with long wings and long tails inhabiting open unenclosed countryside. **Hen Harriers** – which are breeding birds of moorland in Scotland, Ireland, northern England and Wales – are widely distributed on coastal marshes and estuaries in winter. Most winter individuals are 'ringtails', i.e. females or first winter birds. They are dark brown above with a small white rump patch and paler below, heavily streaked, with barred underwings and a strongly three-barred tail. Hen Harriers fly buoyantly, low over the ground, changing direction deftly and alternating short sequences of flapping flight with stiff glides on V-shaped wings; they are agile and dexterous on the wing.

The **Montagu's Harrier** is very similar to the Hen Harrier but is exclusively a summer visitor, now extremely rare and breeding in only one or two lowland areas. It also occurs as a scarce passage bird mainly on downland and coastal levels in May and Aug.-Sept. Both sexes have a delightfully buoyant, almost ethereal, flight and are the smallest and lightest of the harriers. Apart from the subtle flight characteristics, the female can be very difficult to tell apart from the female Hen Harrier. She is narrower-winged and slighter than the Hen Harrier and her white rump patch is very small – often only just visible – but this is not a reliable identification feature on its own. The male has a dirty greyish rump patch (compare Hen Harrier) and prominent black bars on the secondaries; the underwings show a few smudgy markings and the flanks are flecked so that the whole appearance is not so 'clean cut' as that of the male Hen Harrier.

The **Marsh Harrier**, also exclusively a summer visitor, is a reed-bed bird, now mainly occurring in only a few wetland sites in East Anglia and as an occasional passage bird elsewhere. It is the heaviest and most bulky of the harriers and nests in reed-beds, where it hunts by quartering a few feet above the reeds and adjacent marshes with a few purposeful wing beats alternating with long wavering glides: it often seems to be close to stalling and drops into the reeds rather clumsily to take prey. It occasionally perches on posts or low bushes. There is no white on the rump. Females are dark plumaged above and below, with a pale head. The dark patch through the eye gives a head pattern similar to the Osprey's (but Osprey has white underparts; see p. 42).

Buzzard
Same scale

Imm.

Golden Eagles (above): immatures are dark brown with distinctive white patches on wings and white basal half of the tail. Adult birds appear all dark.

White-tailed Eagle (above): note the short wedge-shaped tail. Below: immature fishing.

Imm.

Hen Harrier
Same scale

Golden Eagle

The **Buzzard** (above and right) soars with rigid upswept wings and fanned tail.

Dark phase

Light phase

Buzzard

Rough-legged Buzzard (above and below): tail pattern, dark belly and carpal patches are important features.

The slim projecting head, three-barred tail and barred wings of the **Honey Buzzard** (below) are diagnostic.

EAGLES AND BUZZARDS

The mountains of Scotland are the home of the majestic **Golden Eagle**. Although a very large bird (wingspan over 2m/6ft), distance often makes it appear smaller and Buzzard-like. Main characters in flight are size, noticeably protruding head, medium-length fan-shaped tail and peerless soaring flight. When soaring, the wings are held in a shallow V and the outer half of the wings can be seen to be slightly narrower than the inner half. Immatures are dark brown with white patches on the wings and inner half of the tail, but these features reduce with age and adult birds appear all-dark. The golden crown and hind neck are difficult to see in the field. It is mainly a mountain species, but some pairs use coastal cliffs.

The **White-tailed Eagle**, recently reintroduced to Scotland, has a small population on the W. coast and islands: it occasionally wanders further south. It is a huge and bulky bird, with a wing span of some 2.7m/9ft, vulture-like in flight profile but with a longish neck. The tail – pure white in adults (five years and over) and all-brown in immatures – is very short and wedge-shaped; wings are long and rectangular with parallel edges (not narrower towards the tip as in Golden Eagle). It soars and glides with wings in a completely flat profile. The heavy-billed head protrudes the same distance as the short tail. It is associated with coastal waters, taking fish and waterfowl, but also scavenging widely on the shore. Individuals often perch on rocks near the shoreline.

The **Buzzard** is the commonest bird of prey in much of N. and W. Britain. It is most familiar in soaring flight above lightly wooded hill country, circling leisurely on broad rigid wings pressed well forward with tail spread. The tail is very short and square and the head projects only a little. Although the Buzzard is basically a medium-brown bird, individuals can show a great range of variety both in colours and patterning; most show numerous barring on tail and wings and often a broad white patch on the base of the primaries on the underwing. The call is a plaintive *"meeoo"*. Buzzards are more often seen perched than other birds of prey, frequently sitting on roadside poles or on the ground in fields.

In winter, small numbers of **Rough-legged Buzzards** occur in Britain, mainly on the E. side. They may cause confusion with common Buzzards because both show great variation of plumage. Most Rough-legged Buzzards are very pale below (first winter birds particularly so) and the wings are longer and narrower than the common Buzzard's. They have white tails with a broad black terminal band. On the underside of the wings, the dark carpal patches are always well defined and the wing-tips very dark against the white underwing. The dark belly patch is also an important feature. When hunting, birds frequently hover on slowly beating wings, unlike the common Buzzard. At close quarters, the head is generally pale and the bill markedly small.

The rare **Honey Buzzard** occurs very sparingly in southern England as a summer visitor. Although actually more closely related to kites than buzzards, it can be confused with the common Buzzard, but has a longer tail and a protruding head. It soars freely and glides with angled wings, flexing the tail in kite fashion.

Below (left to right): White-tailed Eagle, Golden Eagle, Buzzard

Osprey

Red Kite

1mm.

1mm.

1mm.

From below, the **Osprey** is
extremely pale; the long wings show a
distinct angle on the leading edge.

The short-winged, long-tailed
silhouette of the soaring
Sparrowhawk (below) is
distinctive, tail spread or closed.
They hunt woodland edge and
hedgerow at low level.

Sparrowhawk

♀

Carrion Crow
Same scale

Adult **Red Kites** have whitish
heads: young birds are browner.
Note the distinctive long forked tail.

Female **Goshawk** is Buzzard
size (compare with Crow);
note 'hooded' impression,
white undertail coverts and
'bulging' secondaries.

Display flight

Goshawks

♀

1mm.

♂

Sparrowhawk ♂

OSPREY, RED KITE, GOSHAWK SPARROWHAWK

Although when seen it is often encountered unexpectedly, the **Osprey** poses few problems of identification. It is a summer visitor and a small population breeds in the Scottish Highlands; however passage birds may appear at freshwater sites anywhere throughout the country in spring and autumn. It is a large bird with long wings (about 1.5m/5ft) a medium length tail and singularly 'loose' wing action. Essentially it has dark brown upperparts and is white below. In flight at a distance it can easily be passed off as a large gull, mainly due to its paleness (undersides) and the arched gull-like attitude of the wings. At closer range note the black carpal patch and the pale head with broad dark stripe through the eye. Ospreys feed on fish caught by plunging feet-first into the water.

The **Red Kite** breeds only in central Wales but wandering individuals and continental migrants regularly appear in other parts, most frequently E. and S. England, although numbers are small. Its plumage is unmistakable, and so too is its flight silhouette. It soars effortlessly on long angled wings (completely different to the stiff-winged attitude of the Buzzard which is so common in areas where Kites are resident) and frequently flexes and twists its long forked russet-coloured tail. It occasionally flaps desultorily, but mainly drifts, soars, hangs and glides with languid facility. It often glides with steeply angled wings. The white patches on the undersides of the wings are very prominent against the blackish primaries. In Wales it inhabits hill country with open sheep-walk, hanging oak woods and small farms. It is most readily seen in winter.

Sparrowhawk and **Goshawk** are very similar woodland species and pose many problems of identification. Confusion easily arises between the two as well as with other birds of prey. Both are long-tailed birds with short rounded wings, barred underparts and tails and similar flight patterns. They are secretive species, often seen only as brief glimpses in wooded country. However, during the breeding season, both species have soaring and diving display flights above their woodlands, and are then at their most visible. Displays involve much wide circling on stiff wings, and spectacular, bounding, deep undulations: the Goshawk is particularly impressive.

The main difference between the species is size, the Goshawk being much the larger, sex for sex; it is important therefore to try to relate the size of a soaring accipiter to other birds, e.g. Crow, Buzzard, Pigeon. Female Sparrowhawks can be as large as male Goshawks, however, which adds to the confusion; female Goshawk is almost Buzzard-sized. Apart from good indications of size, if available, the best feature is the pure white under-tail coverts of the Goshawk (sexes similar) which are dazzlingly evident in display. For finer points, note the bulging curve of the secondaries on the Goshawk and its hooded appearance due to dark ear coverts. The female Sparrowhawk is extremely similar to Goshawk but the male much less so, partly because of its small size and partly on account of its rufous-barred underparts – when visible. Both are forest or woodland species; the Goshawk, until recently very rare, is now re-establishing itself in several areas of the country.

Stoop

Peregrine

Stoop

Soaring flight

Imm.

The **Peregrine** illustrates the classic 'falcon' silhouette. When soaring, the tail is broader than at other times. In level flight, fast shallow wing beats alternate with long glides. The hunting stoop is at awesome speed.

Swifts

Hobby

Pipit

♂

♀

Merlin

Merlin ♂

The **Hobby** (above) is a lowland falcon, long, slender and very fast. It can even outfly swifts.

The tiny **Merlin** (above) has a fast low-level hunting flight in open country.

The widespread **Kestrel** (below) is our commonest falcon. Its hovering flight is familiar – often above motorway verges.

♂

Kestrel

♂

♀

Hovering

All falcon species have pointed wings (although they can look deceptively broader on occasions) and longish tails. Most can fly at impressive speed, and wing beats, though rapid, are very shallow.

The **Peregrine** is the largest of the British falcons (excepting the vagrant Gyr Falcon from the Arctic). It breeds on coastal and inland cliffs, notably in the W. and N. and some winter in the lowlands, particularly on coastal marshes. The classic falcon silhouette is epitomised in the Peregrine, with its solid compact shape rightly giving the impression of great power. The wings and tail are proportionately somewhat shorter than in the other falcons. Peregrines prey on other birds in flight, which they catch either by flying them down with sheer speed or by killing them at the end of a powerful stoop. Perched or at closer range, the fine black barring of the underparts can be seen, as can the black-hooded appearance with prominent moustachial stripe. Immatures are similarly patterned but browner. Peregrines are noisy and active near breeding sites: the call is a loud penetrating *"kek, kek, kek..."*. Sexes are alike, but the female is often much larger than the male.

The **Hobby** is a trans-Saharan migrant breeding thinly but widely in southern counties on downland, heaths and open farmland where pairs can be very difficult to locate. Highly aerial falcons, they are slim and agile with scythe-like wings and an almost Swift-like outline. They hunt other birds – especially hirundines and Swifts – in dashing flight, sometimes after an aerobatic chase, taking prey with a final electric burst of speed; they also feed on large insects (such as crane-flies and dragonflies), often as dusk approaches, in steadier low-level 'hawking' flight. Immature birds (late summer and autumn) are much browner above and lack the rufous thighs. Hobbies can be very unobtrusive much of the time on their breeding grounds and are most obvious during soaring and diving displays early in their season (May). Sexes are alike but the male is brighter.

The diminutive **Merlin** is the least distinctive of the falcons – quick and elusive, often giving only brief views, and thereby confusable with such as Kestrel, Sparrowhawk, pigeons or even Cuckoo. They appear all-dark at a distance and patterning is difficult to see. The blue-grey male has a black terminal band on the tail, and the larger female has a cream-and-brown barred tail. The Merlin is a resident bird, breeding on open moorland and wintering in lowland agricultural areas and coastal marshes and dunes. Flight is dashing and erratic, at low level, in pursuit of small passerines or waders. It is usually very elusive on breeding moors and more readily seen in winter.

The **Kestrel** is the most familiar of our four regular falcons. A small, slender falcon with long narrow wings and long tail, it is common on agricultural land and regular in urban areas and along motorways, where its hovering hunting-flight is well known. Sexes differ: the smaller male has head, rump and tail dove grey, a spotted chestnut mantle and a broad black band near the end of the white-tipped tail. The female's upperparts are duller brown and heavily barred to give a chequered appearance. The tail is similarly barred with a dark band near the creamy tip.

Red Grouse

♀ Summer

Ptarmigan

Winter ♂

Red Grouse (above and top left): both sexes are dark red-brown; male has prominent red wattles.

Ptarmigan (above): sexes are alike in winter but note male's red wattle and small black face patch. Summer female is cryptically camouflaged.

Black Grouse

Blackcock

Capercaillie ♀

Female **Capercaillie** is smaller than male, cryptically coloured with noticeable chestnut chest band.

The **Blackcock's** silhouette (left) distinguishes it from any other bird. Black Grouse often feed incongruously perched in trees.

Capercaillie

The four British grouse species are all upland birds, two open-hill species (Red Grouse and Ptarmigan) and two forest or forest-edge species (Capercaillie, Black Grouse).

The **Red Grouse** feeds largely on heather shoots and is therefore virtually exclusive to tracts of upland heather moor and particularly numerous on the Scottish uplands and Pennines. It is a dark red-brown bird with even darker wings most frequently seen when disturbed from heather; it then rockets up and flies fast, gliding on bowed wings and often tilting from side to side before landing. Coveys are on the wing from July. Cock's breeding-season call is a strident *"go back, go back, bak, bak.."*. Birds crouch in the heather to avoid detection by predators; when on the ground they are most likely to be seen stretching up to peer cautiously over the heather.

Smaller than the Red Grouse, the **Ptarmigan** is confined to the highest Scottish hills, above the altitude at which Red Grouse occur. Birds are often extremely tame and approachable, relying for safety on near perfect cryptic patterning at all seasons (they have three different seasonal plumages). In summer the female's mottled tawny plumage blends perfectly with the moss, lichens, low plants and pebbles of the bare mountain tops. Breeding males are darker grey-brown and black above with fine white vermiculations, pure white below and have red wattles. Autumn males are much paler and greyer, freely suffused with white and showing black centres to many of the upper body feathers. Both sexes are unmistakable in flight at all seasons with pure white wings.

The male **Black Grouse** (Blackcock) is a large bird, readily identified by its glossy black plumage, uniquely shaped tail and white underwing; in flight it shows bold white bars on the upper wing. The smaller Greyhen is cryptically coloured grey-brown with black markings. In forest areas where both species occur she may be confused with female Capercaillie but is smaller and the uniform colouring (compare Capercaillie's rufous breast), forked tail and pale wing bars help to distinguish – but the latter two features are not always easy to see. Female has the same distinctive white underwing as male. They perch and feed freely in trees and often fly higher than Red Grouse, with longer glides when out of danger. Black Grouse inhabit large forest clearings, young plantations and moorland edges. They are now scarce in Wales and N. England but fairly common in Scotland.

In the eastern highlands of central Scotland the huge **Capercaillie** lives in the remnants of old pine forest and also occupies modern conifer plantations. Males are unmistakable: huge turkey-like birds, dark-plumaged and broad-tailed; they have an unusual white spot on the carpal joint. They feed on the forest floor (spring and summer) and also in the crowns of pines (winter). When flushed from the silence of the forest they rise with alarming noise and fly fast through trees for a short way, powerful flapping alternating with long glides: surprisingly agile for so large a bird; also a nimble climber. In flight, females are buff above and pale below with rufous tails and show white patches on the underwing. Barred, rounded tails and chestnut chest-band separate females from the Greyhen.

Pheasant ♀

Pheasant ♂

The long tail feathers on both sexes, and the bright plumage of the male, identify the **Pheasant** easily.

Lady Amherst's Pheasant ♂

Golden Pheasant ♂

Grey Partridge

The **Grey Partridge** (above) is slightly smaller and finer than the **Red-legged Partridge** (below). The latter has a stronger face pattern; the white eye-stripe is visible even from behind.

Red-legged Partridge

Quail (below): sometimes heard, seldom seen. Note male's dark throat stripes and the female's spotted breast.

♀

PARTRIDGES, PHEASANTS, QUAIL

The familiar bright and showy **Pheasant** was introduced into Britain from Asia as early as the 11th century. The white neck-ring on the male is characteristic of the Chinese race but the earliest introductions were from Asia Minor, which race has no neck-ring. Even the dun-coloured females are easy to distinguish by their general shape and long pointed tails. Birds often run for cover in preference to flying. The male has a loud, sudden, crowing call: *"Korr-kok"* usually followed by brief, noisy whirring of wings: this crowing is audible for up to a mile. Pheasants are at home in woodland, agricultural land, reed-beds and even open moorland.

Several other pheasant species are now living wild in parts of Britain, most frequently in lowland England. Of these the **Golden Pheasant** and **Lady Amherst's Pheasant** are the most likely to be encountered. Females are very similar but the female Golden Pheasant has larger more strongly barred tail and Lady Amherst's has a darker rufous crown and greater contrast between the pale background colour and dark barring of the tail.

Two species of partridges occur in Britain (only the Grey Partridge in Ireland). They are dumpy rounded birds, smaller than pheasants, and usually associated with lowland agriculture. They walk with a hunched 'neckless' attitude and crouch when alarmed, but they can run fast, especially the **Red-legged Partridge**. Sexes are alike in this species, which has red legs and feet and strong distinctive patterning on head and flanks: the patterning (especially the white throat) is visible in flight. It has a remarkable chugging 'song'; *"chukka, chukka, chukka…"*, sometimes improbably delivered from a high song-post such as a barn roof or bale stack.

On the ground the indigenous **Grey Partridge** shows a chestnut-orange face and grey breast quite unlike the Red-legged: legs and feet are blue-grey and the male has a brown horseshoe-shaped mark on the pale belly which is indistinct or even absent on the female. Otherwise, the male is slightly brighter and marginally larger. Despite the colours and pattern, partridges merge cryptically with ground colours when they crouch. In flight, both species have fanned chestnut tails and can be difficult to distinguish especially when flying away. Family parties stay together from July to January or February often in coveys of up to 15. The male Grey Partridge has a hoarse 'rusty-gate' call *"karr-ik"* and birds often produce a rapid *"kek, kek, kek"* when flushed. It never uses elevated perches in the way that the Red-legged does.

The tiny **Quail** (18cm/7in) is by far the smallest of our game birds. It is a summer visitor only and numbers vary from year to year; usually it is a very scarce breeding bird but in occasional years quite plentiful, especially on the chalk hills of southern England. The Quail is a bird of hayfields, corn crops and rough pastures, seldom seen but occasionally heard. The call of the male, notably around dusk and dawn (May-July) is a ventriloquial trisyllabic *"whit, pu-whit"* (often aptly likened to *"whet mi-lips"*). Should this elusive bird ever make the mistake of being seen, it resembles a miniature partridge – rotund with streaked plumage and strong head pattern. Flight is partridge-like but slower and usually only over a short distance – like a tennis ball on whirring wings.

Water Rails have a feeble-looking flight with legs dangling.

Water Rail

The **Water Rail** (above) is the only marsh bird with a long reddish bill; note the heavily mottled upperparts, pinkish-brown legs and whitish undertail coverts: swims well when necessary.

Spotted Crake

The **Spotted Crake** (above) has distinctive spotted plumage and well barred flanks. The under-tail coverts are buffish – not white (compare Water Rail) – and this is a diagnostic feature.

Corncrake

Corncrakes (above) will often call from the smallest areas of cover. Flight pattern shows chestnut wings and strongly streaked back.

Moorhen (below) has dark plumage, red frontal shield and green legs.

Co... Im...

Coots are quarrelsome birds of the open water. Immatures are grey above and white below.

Coots

Chick

RAILS AND CRAKES

The **Water Rail** is a skulking bird of reed-beds, swamps and similar wet areas associated with slow-moving water. In winter it spreads more widely, also using ditches, ponds, sewage farms etc. Smaller than a Moorhen, it differs from all other marshland birds in having a long bill. It can move lithely and surprisingly quickly through stems at the base of the reed-bed. It has streaked brown upperparts and slaty blue-grey underparts with black and white barring on flanks. Immature birds are less well marked and lack the grey underparts. Individuals will emerge shyly to feed in the open when all is very quiet, so look for birds on soft mud at the marsh edge or scuttling back into cover, flicking the tail to show whitish under-tail coverts in the same way as a Moorhen does. At other times the birds will move with high-stepping gait or in an easy loping run. More often heard than seen. Water Rails produce a wide range of groans, grunts and squeals, from the depths of the marshy vegetation, often blood chilling in their effect.

The rare **Spotted Crake** breeds very sparingly throughout Britain in bogs and tangled swamps but is exceedingly elusive. Much the same size as the Water Rail, it appears to be smaller because of the much shorter bill. Its voice is distinctive, likened to a repeated whiplash at the rate of more than one a second – *"hewitt"*; the call is uttered from dusk onwards into the night through spring and summer. The male also has a Snipe-like *"tik-tok"* call sometimes produced endlessly and monotonously. Usually solitary. Although a few birds may over-winter it is mainly a summer visitor.

Like the two former species, the **Corncrake** is more likely to be heard than seen. It is now a rare summer visitor with reducing strongholds in the Hebrides and Ireland. It is a secretive bird of hayfields and damp grassy places. The call is an endless, penetrating two-note rasping sound, *"crek-crek...crek-crek...crek-crek"*. The flight looks weak and reluctant – Moorhen-like with legs trailing – although as with other crakes this is obviously deceptive in view of the distances it migrates. 'Singing' birds can be lured into view by immitating the call, either vocally or with a small stick along the teeth of a comb.

The **Moorhen** is one of the commonest and most familiar of our waterside birds, an inhabitant of still waters and slow-moving rivers in town and countryside. Moorhens swim with a characteristically jerky head movement and when alarmed retreat to the nearest cover with feet pattering on the surface or in low flight with legs trailing. They do not dive like Coots, but have a knack of 'disappearing' (often by partially submerging) when they swim into the shelter of the bank. Moorhens feed on land as well as water and run for cover flirting the tail to display white under coverts. Moorhen nests can often be seen amid reed stems in the water and sometimes in overhanging bushes.

The **Coot** is an inhabitant of larger open waters than those habitually used by the Moorhen. The white frontal shield is very evident on the all-black plumage. Coots swim farther out into more open water when disturbed not (like Moorhen) into bankside cover. They dive for food from the surface and are fairly noisy and aggressive birds.

Curlew (above): females often have distinctly longer bills than males. Both Curlew and Whimbrel (right) show a white V on the rump in flight.

Curlew

♀

♂

Imm.

Whimbrel

Whimbrel (above) are darker than Curlew, with different bill shape and size, supercilium and faster wing beats.

Winter

Spring

Black-tailed Godwits

Black-tailed Godwits have conspicuous white wing bars and white tails with a broad terminal black band. Note that the legs protrude well beyond the tail.

Spring

The **Bar-tailed Godwit** (below) is shorter-legged and has a distinctly up-curved bill. The flight pattern is completely different; note the unmarked wings, white V up the back (compare Curlew, Whimbrel, Greenshank) and shorter legs.

Spring

Winter

Bar-tailed Godwit

Waders as a group pose many problems of identification – the many very similar species; the distances at which they are often viewed; the complexity of seasonal occurrences as well as some seasonal plumage variations etc. Many species are long-distance migrants moving between breeding gounds in the Arctic and wintering areas in southern Europe and Africa. Many occurrences in Britain are therefore transitory, principally in spring and autumn but complicated by non-breeding (summering) individuals and small numbers of over-wintering individuals of species mainly travelling much further south.

In identifying waders, bear in mind various factors, including calls, behaviour, habitat, wing and tail patterns, as well as size and basic plumage details. Several 'accidentals' or vagrants occur annually in Britain and, of these, the Pectoral Sandpiper (pp. 62-63) from North America is the most regular.

Of the larger waders, the **Curlew** is a common and familiar bird, breeding in lowland meadows and on the uplands, and wintering in large flocks mainly on estuaries and coastal marshes. Its very long, gently curved bill is only likely to be confused with Whimbrel (below), but young Curlews do not have fully developed bills until late autumn. Flight is rather gull-like when travelling any distance but more floating and lazy over the breeding ground. The beautiful spring 'song' is liquid and rippling, often starting with slow "*coor-li*" notes, building up repetitively to a bubbling crescendo. The clear "*coor-li*" call is used throughout the year.

The **Whimbrel** is similar in appearance to Curlew but smaller and darker, with a shorter, more decurved bill. It is a spring and autumn migrant and a small number breed on moorlands in the far N. of Scotland, especially the northern islands. The Whimbrel's flight pattern is similar to Curlew's but wing beats are quicker and the dark supercilium and pale stripe through the eye are often visible at a considerable range. The tittering call of (usually seven) rippling, evenly emphasised notes is very distinctive; used particularly on spring passage.

Two species of godwits winter around our shores and large numbers pass through on passage in spring and autumn. A few **Black-tailed Godwits** may also turn up inland, where small numbers breed on water meadow sites (e.g. the Ouse Washes in Norfolk/Cambs.). The Black-tailed is the larger of the two godwits, longer-legged and with a virtually straight bill. In non-breeding plumage and at long distance they can be difficult to separate but at closer range the Black-tailed has a more noticeable supercilium and uniform upperparts. Although both godwits are alike in winter plumage, once in flight confusion is impossible because of the very different tail and wing patterns (see opposite).

The **Bar-tailed Godwit** is a passage and wintering bird on British coasts (a few summer). The dull buffish winter plumage is uniform except that, at close range, the upperparts are lightly streaked. Flighting flocks sometimes indulge in whirling, synchronous aerobatics. Some spring passage birds may be seen in breeding dress: females are usually much as in winter but males change into varying degrees of brick-red on underparts, head and neck.

Golden Plover are richly gold-spangled in summer (below); black belly is lost in winter.

The **Grey Plover** (below and left) has spangled grey plumage, fairly large head and eye and heavy bill. Black 'wing-pits' are diagnostic in flight (Golden's are white).

The **Lapwing's** tumbling display flight and wild "pee-wit" calling in spring are unmistakable. Outside the breeding season, face is buff above cheek line.

Summer plumaged **Dotterel** (left), on spring passage, are bright and distinctive. Females are larger and brighter than males. Autumn adults and immatures are less conspicuous.
Ringed Plover (below): leg and bill colour are diagnostic in summer. Winter birds may lack black forehead band. White wing bar distinguishes it from Little Ringed Plover in flight.

The **Little Ringed Plover** (below) has pale legs, a yellow eye-ring and a thin white line above the black forecrown. Note the black bill.

Golden Plover

Imm.

Lapwing

Winter

Spring

S. Race

N. Race

♀

♂

Grey Plover

Imm.

Winter

♀ Dotterel

Imm.

Ringed Plover

Imm.

Little Ringed Plover

The **Lapwing** breeds widely throughout Britain. In winter, it congregates into large flocks in lowland fields and coastal marshes. It is our only wader with a crest. In flight it appears essentially dark above and white below and has broad rounded wings. The dark upperparts have a strong purple and/or green sheen. The call – a strident *"pee-wit"* – is used throughout the year, but birds are particularly vocal in spring.

The **Golden Plover** often associates with Lapwing flocks on inland or coastal fields in winter, but it is not a shoreline bird. In summer they breed on the high moors. At all seasons, the dark upperparts are strongly speckled with gold and in the breeding season the chest and belly are black; northern breeding birds show much more black. Flight is rapid, on long narrow wings which show a faint wing bar. When landing, they often hold their wings up before settling showing white wing-linings. When feeding, birds characteristically run a few steps, then pause. On the moors where they breed, the male's evocative call is a plaintive, fluting *"poor-ri"*; the normal call is a single *"peee"*.

The **Grey Plover** closely resembles the Golden Plover in shape, size and pattern but is a little larger and sturdier. There is no overlap in habitat, however, as the Grey Plover is exclusively a shoreline bird. It is a winter visitor and passage migrant. The long, narrow wings show a thin white bar above and the rump is white. On the shore, the birds feed well spaced out and have a characteristic run-and-pause hunting method. The call is a plaintive double note *"peeoowee"*.

Dotterel breed on the high mountains of Europe, including Scotland, and occur in small numbers inland on passage in May and Sept.-Oct., faithfully using the same fields or hill tops as stopping places. They are very confiding and approachable. Autumn birds are superficially similar to Golden Plover but smaller and immediately identifiable by the white supercilia, which meet at the back of the head to produce a white V. The legs are pale yellow. Dotterel do not associate with water. In flight they are distinctly dark bellied during the breeding season.

Ringed Plovers are common coastal birds, present all year. Some breed inland, especially in Scotland and northern England and many Arctic breeders pass north in May, returning in late summer. Confusion is unlikely with any other species except Little Ringed Plover (exclusively an inland bird and summer visitor); Ringed Plovers often occur at inland waters on migration. The Ringed Plover has orange legs (but beware when they are muddy!) and in flight shows a marked white wing bar. The flight call is a gentle *"too-li"*. Young birds show only shadowy head markings and the pale edges to the feathers produce a scaly appearance.

Little Ringed Plovers occur as summer visitors (Mar.-Sept.) to freshwater sites on reservoirs, shingly river banks and gravel pits in the southern half of the country. It is smaller and slighter than the Ringed Plover and less extrovert in its behaviour. The lack of any noticeable wing bar is an important character for separating from Ringed Plover in flight. Note the eye-ring at close range. The high-pitched *"pee-u"* call is totally different from Ringed Plover's.

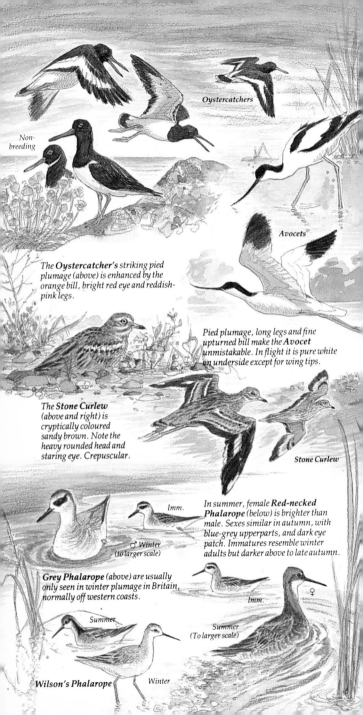

Oystercatchers

Non-breeding

Avocets

The **Oystercatcher's** *striking pied plumage (above) is enhanced by the orange bill, bright red eye and reddish-pink legs.*

*Pied plumage, long legs and fine upturned bill make the **Avocet** unmistakable. In flight it is pure white on underside except for wing tips.*

The **Stone Curlew** *(above and right) is cryptically coloured sandy brown. Note the heavy rounded head and staring eye. Crepuscular.*

Stone Curlew

Imm.

♂ *Winter (to larger scale)*

*In summer, female **Red-necked Phalarope** (below) is brighter than male. Sexes similar in autumn, with blue-grey upperparts, and dark eye patch. Immatures resemble winter adults but darker above to late autumn.*

Grey Phalarope *(above) are usually only seen in winter plumage in Britain, normally off western coasts.*

Imm.

♀

Summer

Summer (To larger scale)

Wilson's Phalarope   *Winter*

OYSTERCATCHER, AVOCET, STONE CURLEW
PHALAROPES

The **Oystercatcher** is the most conspicuous of seashore waders, inhabiting both low coasts and cliff slopes. Apart from its coastal distribution throughout the year – with some areas holding very large flocks in winter – the Oystercatcher also breeds inland near water in Scotland and northern England; elsewhere it is occasionally found inland on passage. This large pied bird with long orange bill is noisy and active. Its strident alarm calls *"kleep, kleep, kleep"* and peculiar communal gatherings of 'piping' birds are familiar features of the seashore. Immatures and winter adults have conspicuous white 'chinstraps'.

The rare **Avocet** is unlikely to be confused with any other species. Small numbers of this elegant wader breed in Norfolk and Suffolk and some winter on the estuaries of south-west England. The pattern of black and white plumage is unique and in flight the long legs trail clearly. The Avocet is a noisy and aggressive species when on its breeding grounds. The call is a far-carrying *"kleep, kleep"*.

On a few sandy heaths, open downs and plains in the south of England, scattered pairs of the strange **Stone Curlew** still breed. The large (40cm/16") summer visitor is not a curlew, as its name suggests, but more akin to the plovers, particularly in its actions. It is a somewhat ungainly bird with a creeping and furtive gait, preferring to crouch with head lowered, relying on its cryptic colouring to avoid detection, or walking away rather than flying. The legs are long but noticeably stout. In flight, the Stone Curlew has distinctive patterning both above and below. It is active at dusk, when it can most readily be located by its loud Curlew-like call, a wailing *"cour-lee"*.

The **Red-necked Phalarope** is a summer visitor which breeds very sparingly in the islands of N. and W. Scotland. In autumn, it occurs very rarely as a passage bird, most usually on the North Sea coasts. This and the Grey Phalarope (see below) are the only two British waders which habitually feed by swimming, classically by spinning around on the water surface to stir up small food items, picking them off with the needle-thin bill. It is a small (Dunlin-sized) wader, reminiscent of a miniature Moorhen when it swims jerkily on the water.

The **Grey Phalarope** nests in the high Arctic and winters at sea, usually passing southwards well offshore. Adverse weather conditions in autumn can cause the birds to be blown onto the western seaboard which is when and where most occur; fewer birds are seen – albeit regularly – on the eastern seaboard. It is therefore only seen in winter plumage in Britain. The Grey Phalarope is a larger and stockier bird then the Red-necked, with a shorter and thicker bill. Identification is further aided by the fact that Red-necked Phalaropes have normally long departed by the time any Grey Phalaropes occur offshore. Young birds have black-brown upper plumage with prominent buff back stripes. By the first winter, these immatures closely resemble adults.

The rare **Wilson's Phalarope** – illustrated opposite – occurs as an annual but scarce vagrant from North America. It is larger than the Grey and lacks the white wing bar of the other two species.

The **Spotted Redshank's** legs are longer, darker and redder than the Redshank's. Note larger slender build and long thin bill. In flight, the white rump patch is a distinctive shape.

Redshank (above): orange-red legs, bill colour and noisy calls distinguish it. Note the diagnostic wing pattern with white trailing edge.

Greenshank (above) are the palest of the large waders, especially in winter, grey above and white below. The bill is slightly upturned and the legs – longer than Redshank's – are pale olive-green.

Common Sandpiper (right): note stiff, bowed wings with white wing bar.

Green Sandpiper (below) is darker than Wood Sandpiper, with larger body but shorter legs. Both have obvious white rumps.

The slender **Wood Sandpiper** (below) has spangled upperparts, pale underwings, a distinct supercilium and different leg colour from the Green.

LARGER SANDPIPERS AND SHANKS

Redshanks are common waders, breeding widely on coastal marshes, damp meadows and boggy uplands, and congregating in large numbers on coasts in winter. They are very noisy and alert birds with a ringing *"teu, yeu, yeu"* call. It is the only common wader with broad white trailing edges to the wings. Redshanks perch more freely than most other waders.

Outside the breeding season, the **Spotted Redshank** is basically similar in colouring to the Redshank, although more grey than brown. There are other important differences: the former is a taller, more graceful bird with a longer straight bill and no clear white on the wings. It has a long white patch on the rump and back and in winter its paler ash-grey upperparts are liberally flecked with white. The call, a loud *"chewit"*, is diagnostic. Breeding-plumaged birds are magnificently coal black, spangled with white on the upperparts but are only seen in Britain in June or July; birds in blotched transitional plumage are more frequent. In autumn, immatures resemble winter adults but have dark grey barring over the underparts. Spotted Redshank nest in N. Scandinavia and USSR and a few winter on British coasts; it is fairly common on passage inland, but more so on coasts (May and July-Oct.).

Greenshank breed sparingly on the moors of N. Scotland (numerously in Scandinavia and USSR) but are best known as passage birds in spring and autumn, both on coasts and inland. A few winter, especially on S. and W. coasts. They are mainly solitary or in small groups. Lanky, pale birds, they are active feeders in shallow waters, often dashing in pursuit of prey. They are wary and nervous. In flight, they have dark, unmarked wings, a long white V up the back (compare Bar-tailed Godwit, Curlew pp. 52-53) and helpfully have a diagnostic ringing call *"tew, tew, tew"*. In winter, the plumage lacks the head and neck streaking of summer and the upperparts too are even paler.

The **Common Sandpiper** is a summer visitor to upland riversides and lakes. Occasional birds overwinter; on passage, it occurs inland and on coasts. Birds fly with stiff bowed wings and a flicking action, low over the water, usually landing on a stone; the flight call is a shrill, staccato *"sweep, seep, seep"*. On waterside shingles they bob all the time in a nervous, jerky manner. The olive-brown upperparts are finely mottled with black.

Both **Green Sandpiper** and **Wood Sandpiper** are freshwater waders, similar in shape and build to the Common Sandpiper, and occurring throughout the country on spring (April-early June) and more numerously on autumn (July-Oct.) passage. A few Green Sandpipers winter. When disturbed, both species rise steeply, especially the Green Sandpiper which starts with a fast zig-zag and then continues climbing higher. It is a darker plumaged bird (including blackish underwings) than the Wood Sandpiper, appearing almost black with the white underparts and rump showing starkly white – often likened to a large House Martin in flight, only with a Snipe-like action. Neither species has wing bars. Calls are very different and often uttered as the birds take flight: the Wood Sandpiper has a rapid and diagnostic *"chiff, chiff, chiff"* whereas the Green Sandpiper has *"kluit-wit-wit"*.

Winter

Summer

Dunlins

Imm.

Curlew Sandpipers

Winter

Winter

Summer

Summer

In winter, identify the **Dunlin** *(above)
by longish bill with down-curved tip and
busy feeding action; often in great
throngs. Summer birds have rich
chestnut on the upperparts and a
distinctive black belly.*

***Curlew Sandpiper** (above): the all-
white rump and grey tail band are
unique among small waders. Note more
elegant proportions than Dunlin. Bill is
longer and more decurved.*

*The **Knot** (below) is a solid looking bird
with short neck and legs and a heavy
straight bill.*

Purple Sandpiper

Summer

Winter

*The **Purple Sandpiper** (above) is a
tame, silent wader with dark plumage,
paler belly and dull yellowish legs.*

*The **Turnstone** (below) has
a lively harlequin pattern:
note bright orange legs.*

Knot

*The **Sanderling** (below and right in
flight) is a very pale bird in winter. In
flight, the white wing bar is broader
than other small waders and the leading
edge darker.*

Winter

Sanderlings

Summer

Winter

Turnstone

Winter

SMALL WADERS: MOSTLY SEEN ON COASTS

Our commonest and most familiar small wader is the **Dunlin**, best known as a coastal bird in winter, often in dense flocks. On passage, scattered birds are not uncommon by inland waters and the British race breeds on upland moors; other northern races occur on passage and in winter. Winter Dunlin are very small waders with brownish-grey upperparts, white underparts (but streaked breast) and black bill and legs. They are busy feeders, often right at the tideline, probing constantly and fast as they move ahead of the rising tide. Autumn immatures have golden brown fringes to feathers on the upperparts and lightly spotted under-parts (until Oct.) and are then the same as winter adults. The slightly rasping flight call *"krri"* distinguishes Dunlin safely from all other waders. On the winter feeding grounds, the birds fly in dense swirling flocks. Dunlin can be confiding and approachable.

The **Curlew Sandpiper** is a rather scarce passage bird, often associating with the slightly smaller Dunlin. Mainly coastal, but occasionally inland. Many passage adults (May and July-Aug.) are in transitional plumage between the grey of winter and brick-red of summer. In autumn, most are immatures with scalier upperparts and lightly streaked buffish breasts. Care is needed to separate them from Dunlin in winter plumage; the Curlew Sandpiper is longer-legged and more elegant with a longer, more decurved bill. Behaviour as Dunlin but not flocking.

The **Purple Sandpiper** is a winter visitor to rocky shores, piers and breakwaters. It is mainly found on N. and W.coasts, where its dark plumage is sometimes difficult to pick out against the dark, wet rocks. They have a squat, rather heavy shape. When feeding, they dodge amongst the spray and breaking waves on the rocks.

The **Knot** is a winter visitor to the largest, sandier estuaries and shorelines, often in great numbers and occupying the same roost sites and feeding areas as Dunlin. Wheeling flocks in the distance look like moving clouds of smoke. The Knot is a sturdy, compact wader half as big again as the Dunlin. In winter plumage, it is grey above and whitish below. In flight, it has a narrow white wing bar, pale rump and pale grey tail. Some spring birds show the bright russet breeding plumage.

Sanderling on passage and in winter prefer wide sandy shores where they often feed on the tide's edge running from each breaking wave with amazing speed – so fast that leg movements cannot be followed. In winter, it is the whitest of small waders, with a prominent black 'shoulder' patch, and black legs, bill and eye. Summer plumaged birds are not unusual, with warm black and chestnut mottled upperparts. Autumn immatures are chequered black and white above. The call is a liquid, conversational *"twik, twik"*, not to be confused with any other British wader call.

The summer **Turnstone** is unmistakable, a tortoiseshell pattern of chestnut, black and white, with a unique head pattern. They are mainly birds of rocky coasts and pebble beaches. They are long-distance spring and autumn migrants but a few over-summer and some may also stay the winter. Passage birds sometimes turn up inland. They feed by poking amongst seaweed, frequently flicking over pebbles. The call is a conversational rippling *"tuc, tuc, tuc"*.

Woodcock

Drumming

Snipe

On the ground, the **Woodcock's** marvellous cryptic patterning (above) makes it almost impossible to see.

The **Jack Snipe** (below) rises silently (Snipe calls): pale stripes contrast strongly against the dark back in flight. Note shorter bill and no white in tail.

The **Snipe** (above) has an enormously long bill. White outer edges of tail help distinguish it from Jack Snipe.

Ruff
Spring

Pectoral Sandpiper (below): note strongly marked upperparts, bold creamy eye-stripe and heavily marked breast sharply separated from pure white underparts.

Imm.

Reeve
Spring

Pectoral Sandpiper

Ruff
Winter

Temminck's Stint (below) has pale legs and almost all-white tail. Note fine pectoral band in summer. **Little Stint** (below right) has short straight bill and black legs.

The **Ruff** and **Reeve** (above): note basic shape, size and flight pattern.

Temminck's Stint
Summer

Winter

Little Stint

Imm.

WADERS MOST LIKELY TO BE SEEN INLAND

The elusive **Woodcock** breeds on the woodland floor, emerging at dusk to feed unseen on the open fields. When disturbed, they rise and fly twisting through the trees, chestnut-coloured and owl-like. The best hope of seeing Woodcock is to look and listen for them at dusk in spring and summer when the males do their 'roding' (courtship) flight over woodland and adjacent fields, calling with a low *"tssip"* preceded by low croaking sounds.

Snipe are most frequently found on inland marshes and water's edge. In spring, breeding birds have an aerial display flight in which the outer tail feathers produce a fast unbirdlike *"burrrrrr"* ('drumming'). At this season the male also has a monotonous *"tik tok"* 'song' uttered either out of sight in marshy ground or sometimes from a post. When flushed, the birds rise with a nasal, rasping *"schaap"* and fast zig-zag flight. They are secretive and usually solitary, but form small flocks in winter. Most likely confusion is with the scarce Jack Snipe.

The **Jack Snipe** is scarcer and even more secretive than the common Snipe, usually seen only when accidentally flushed underfoot. Its flight is then less urgent than Snipe's without the exaggerated zig-zagging, and it often drops back into cover a short distance away. Winter visitor only, to wet meadows and muddy areas. Silent when flushed.

For a few short weeks in spring, the male **Ruff** sports an amazing array of head and neck feathers (which can vary enormously in colour). The Ruff breeds very sparingly on wet meadows, otherwise it is a fairly numerous inland and coastal passage bird on muddy areas, chiefly in late summer and autumn. It is a Redshank-sized bird, somewhat heavy-bodied and small-headed with a dark medium-length bill. The male is 5cm/2" larger than the female (Reeve). Immatures have scaly sandy-coloured upperparts with dark centres to the feathers giving a mosaic effect, and buffish unmarked breasts: winter adults are similar but more greyish-white. Even the leg colour varies from green and greyish to brown, orange or reddish.

The **Pectoral Sandpiper** is the most regular of 'accidental' waders to reach our shores each year. A North American bird, it turns up on inland wetland sites in Aug.-Oct. It is larger than Dunlin, with a protruding breast, and sometimes stretches upwards, recalling a small Reeve. In flight, the upper wing is virtually unmarked, showing only an indistinct bar.

Temminck's Stint and **Little Stint** are our smallest waders, about 5cm/2" shorter than the Dunlin, with short straight bills. The Little Stint mainly occurs as a passage bird, Aug.-Oct., associating with Dunlin and other small waders. The flight pattern is Dunlin-like but young birds (which predominate) show two distinct Vs on their backs. It is an energetic bird, scampering and foraging ceaselessly. Winter colours are essentially brown-grey above and white below. Temminck's Stint is an uncommon autumn passage bird, by inland waters. It has an elongated profile from Little Stint, shorter pale legs and well marked breast; little seasonal change in plumage. It rises high and fast – Snipe-like – when flushed. Almost always solitary.

Gannets

Imm.

Fulmar

Size and dazzling white plumage (top) make adult **Gannets** unmistakable; immatures have brown-and-white harlequin plumage becoming whiter over 3-4 years.

The **Fulmar** (above) has silvery-grey wings, back and tail and pure white head and underparts. They often play in the updraughts of breeding cliffs.

Leach's Petrel

Storm Petrel

Manx Shearwaters (above) low over the sea.

The **Shag** is a smaller slimmer bird than Cormorant, with a whispy tuft of head feathers in spring. Immatures are brown – no white underparts as in Cormorant.

The **Storm Petrel** (above) follows behind boats well out at sea with a weak pattering flight but also has a more purposeful flight.
The **Cormorant** (below) swims very low with neck upright and bill tilted upwards. Adults have a white thigh patch in spring.

Imm.

Shag

Spring

Winter

Diver

Imm. Cormorant

Cormorant

'Drying' posture

The **Gannet** is the largest seabird in the North Atlantic and unmistakable in adult plumage. It is regular offshore, occasionally with large congregations gathering to dive spectacularly into shoaling fish. Well known colonies are on Grassholm (Wales), Flamborough Head (Humberside), Bass Rock (Firth of Forth) and Ailsa Craig (Ayrshire). Young birds are dark brown flecked with white and become progressively whiter over four years until maturity.

The **Manx Shearwater** breeds in colonies on marine islands off the western seaboard. During spring and summer they are frequently to be seen from headlands in loose parties passing offshore and they congregate in big 'rafts' on the sea near colonies in the evenings. The sharp contrast between black upperparts and white underside makes them relatively easy to pick out as they plane low over the surface of the waves on long narrow wings with intermittent wing beats, rising and falling over the troughs. At the breeding colonies – often very large – the birds are strictly nocturnal to avoid predation by large gulls. In late summer it is worth sea-watching for rarer shearwaters: the larger **Great Shearwater** has a black cap, white rump patch and 'collar' and the **Sooty Shearwater** is heavy-looking and appears all-black at a distance although the pale wing-linings 'flash' as the bird careens and banks. Both plane in similar ways to the Manx Shearwater.

Although initially gull-like in appearance, especially in its size and colouring, the long narrow wings, planing flight and masterly aerial control of the **Fulmar** quickly distinguish it from all other seabirds. It glides supremely, often at speed, with one wing tip barely skimming the surface of the sea. Birds often inquisitively approach the observer on the cliff top, passing very close on the updraughts and 'holding' on the wind using feet as rudders. It nests on sheer sea-cliffs and colonies can be very large.

The tiny **Storm Petrel** comes to land – on remote western islands – only to nest; otherwise it lives far out at sea and is seldom seen from the mainland. The rarer **Leach's Petrel** is slightly larger and has a distinctive bounding flight and no white underwing patches; its forked tail is an insignificant field character. The Storm Petrel regularly follows ships at sea whereas the Leach's does not.

Comorants are dark plumaged birds which fish inshore waters and are also frequently found inland on rivers and reservoirs, especially outside the breeding season: less marine than the Shag. Often confused at a distance with divers (pp. 16-19) but the profiles show important differences (see opposite). Separation from Shag is not always easy especially involving young birds, although the Cormorant is in fact much bigger and heavier. Note the white chin patch of adult and the heavy, hook-tipped yellow bill. Flight is puposeful and direct with head unusually held above the horizontal. Many of their movements are distinctly reptilian.

The **Shag** is usually found off rocky coasts, also occurring further out at sea (stacks and reefs) than the Cormorant. Adults look all-black at a distance with a prominent yellow patch at base of bill. They have a slim neck and an apologetic tuft of crest feathers (adult) in spring. Immature birds are pale brown below and show no white. They surface dive with an arched jump.

Winter

Herring Gulls

Imm.

Summer

Lesser Black-backed Imm.

Herring Gull Winter

Common Gulls

Summer

Imm. Common Gull. Note tail pattern.

Common Gull Winter

The adult **Herring Gull** (top) has a silver-grey mantle and wings and pink legs. Note uniform colouring of immature's tail base, rump and mantle (compare Lesser Black-backed).

Common Gull (above and left): note greenish yellow legs, rounder head, neater bill and smaller size than Herring Gull. Adults' heads are streaked grey in winter, not in summer; Herring Gull less streaked.

Lesser Black-backed's wings are long and narrow (right); note how far they project beyond the tail. Head very streaked in winter. Note pale rump of immature, compared to mantle and tail base. Primaries are all dark.

Large size, pink legs and dark grey back identify the **Great Black-backed** (below). The head remains unstreaked in winter.

Lesser Black-backed

Great Black-backed

Imm.

Great Black-ba

This is a large group with several similar species and many problems and pitfalls of identification. Plumage changes are very complex, particularly in the transitional stages between juvenile and adult, often taking several years (five for Herring and Black-backed for example, and three for the Common Gull). In the following accounts only adult and first winter plumages are covered. Sexes are alike in all species. Size of bird, leg colour, bill shape, pattern, size, colour, and wing patterns in flight are the most important factors to note.

The **Herring Gull** is the most common and familiar seaside gull found everywhere round coasts but also inland on rubbish dumps, reservoirs etc. Adult birds are all white except for silver-grey back and wings which are tipped black and white. Note leg colour and bill pattern. The eye has a yellow/orange orbital ring which gives a deeply malevolent look to the bird. The two other common gulls with grey backs and black wing tips are Kittiwake and Common Gull (see below and pp. 68-69 for differences). First winter birds are particularly difficult to separate from Lesser Black-backs but have inner primaries which are paler than the outer ones, producing a distinctive wing pattern. They also tend to have tail base, rump and mantle a uniform colour whereas the Lesser Black-back's rump is noticeably paler. The laughing call is the traditional 'seagull's cry', so evocative of the seaside.

The **Common Gull** breeds in Scotland, northern England and Ireland and winters throughout Britain where it is often found on farmland, playing fields etc. It is smaller than the Herring Gull, which is similarly patterned, but the Common Gull has a neater, rounder head and smaller bill. The bluer-grey back makes it look strikingly white-headed and the black wing tips have prominent white 'mirrors'; the leg colour is diagnostic. First winter birds have a broad black band on otherwise white tail and the brown mantle of immature plumage becomes grey by autumn. First winter birds are very similar to the rare Mediterranean Gull (see overleaf) which has a paler mantle, darker legs and bill and almost unmarked underwing coverts (mottled in the Common Gull).

The **Lesser Black-backed Gull** has a dark grey back and yellow legs. It is Herring Gull sized, but slimmer and more elegant, and very similar to the larger, darker-backed Great Black-backed Gull. The grey tone of the back is variable, especially in winter when some birds of the Scandinavian race occur and they are almost as dark as Great Black-backs. Birds in first winter plumage are darker than both Great Black-backs and Herring Gulls of the same age. They are separable with care from the very similar Herring Gulls (see above). The Lesser Black-backed is a widespread coastal gull, also occuring inland on passage and in winter.

The **Great Black-backed Gull** is the largest of all the gulls, with a nearly black mantle and wings, and pink legs. Size alone usually determines this gull but at a distance it may be mistaken for Lesser Black-backed. Juveniles and first winter birds have whiter heads and paler upperparts than other large gulls, and are much bigger with very large black bills. This gull is common on western coasts; less so in the east and inland. Voice is a deep, clipped *"kwow"*

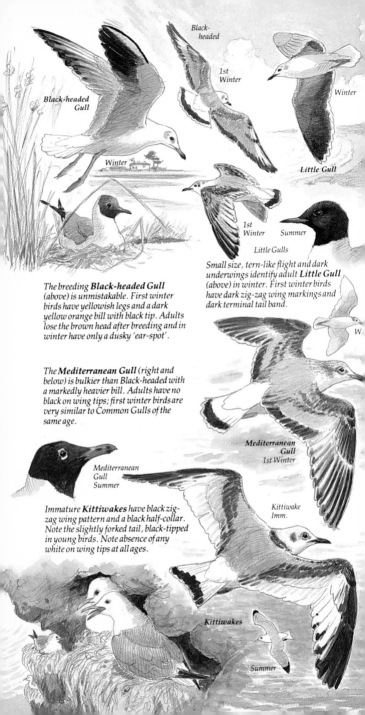

The breeding **Black-headed Gull** (above) is unmistakable. First winter birds have yellowish legs and a dark yellow orange bill with black tip. Adults lose the brown head after breeding and in winter have only a dusky 'ear-spot'.

Small size, tern-like flight and dark underwings identify adult **Little Gull** (above) in winter. First winter birds have dark zig-zag wing markings and dark terminal tail band.

The **Mediterranean Gull** (right and below) is bulkier than Black-headed with a markedly heavier bill. Adults have no black on wing tips; first winter birds are very similar to Common Gulls of the same age.

Immature **Kittiwakes** have black zig-zag wing pattern and a black half-collar. Note the slightly forked tail, black-tipped in young birds. Note absence of any white on wing tips at all ages.

Black-headed

Black-headed
Gull

1st
Winter

Winter

Little Gull

Winter

1st
Winter   Summer

Little Gulls

W

Mediterranean
Gull
1st Winter

Mediterranean
Gull
Summer

Kittiwake
Imm.

Kittiwakes

Summer

GULLS: KITTIWAKE AND GULLS WITH BLACK HEADS IN SUMMER

The **Little Gull** is the world's smallest gull, only about Mistle Thrush size. It breeds in eastern Europe and Russia and is normally only an autumn and winter visitor in small but increasing numbers. Individuals sometimes linger in summer: very occasionally, pairs have bred. They feed from the water surface with an agile, tern-like flight. In winter the adults are all-pale above with only a small dusky 'ear-spot' (similar to Black-headed Gull) plus a blackish cap. Young birds have prominent zig-zag markings on the upper wing (see also Kittiwake below), pale pink legs and tiny black bill; by late autumn the brown back has given way to pale grey of the first-winter plumage. Adults have completely blackish underwings, which are diagnostic, but first winter birds have pale underwings.

The **Black-headed Gull** is the most familiar inland gull, although it is equally found round the coasts. It uses farmland – often following the plough – inland waters, playing fields, town centres, refuse tips etc. It is a smallish gull with a dark brown hood in summer (not black as the name implies) and red legs, bill and eye-ring. In winter the legs and feet are brighter and the bill is tipped with black; the dark hood is lost and only a smoky dark 'ear-spot' remains. In flight in all plumages there is a clear white leading edge to the wings, visible from both below and above, which distinguishes this gull from any other. First winter birds are pale-headed and pale-bodied with patterned wings which still show the white leading edge. The square-ended tail has a dark terminal band. Black-headed Gulls are particularly dexterous on the wing, with an easy, buoyant and agile flight.

The **Mediterranean Gull** is bulkier than the similar-sized Black-headed Gull. It breeds mainly in the Black Sea area and winters in the Mediterranean; individuals increasingly reach British shores, mainly to S. and E. coasts. First winter birds are likely to be confused with Black-headed (with which they freely consort), especially at rest. However the young Mediterranean Gulls look bulkier, with broader wings, deeper bills, longer legs and darker wingtips. In flight, confusion with immature Common Gulls (see previous page) is particularly likely as the wing patterns are very similar; the Mediterranean Gull is a little smaller and has a paler back and dark mask. Adult birds are immediately distinguished by the lack of black on wing tips, white underwings and, in summer, the jet black hood and white eye-ring.

The **Kittiwake** is the most marine of our gulls living far out to sea except when coming to coastal cliffs to breed in large, densely-packed colonies; it is only seen inland when storm-blown. Kittiwakes are intermediate in size between Common and Black-headed Gulls. The most important features of the adults are the grey mantle and wings, all white body, head and tail (all similar to Common Gull) and solid black – 'dipped-in-ink' – wing tips with no white spots or other markings. The grey of the upper wings is paler on the outer parts of the wings, unlike any other gull. At the colonies the repeated, strident *"Kittiwaak"* calls are diagnostic. Note the lemon yellow bill, black legs and red eye-ring at close range.

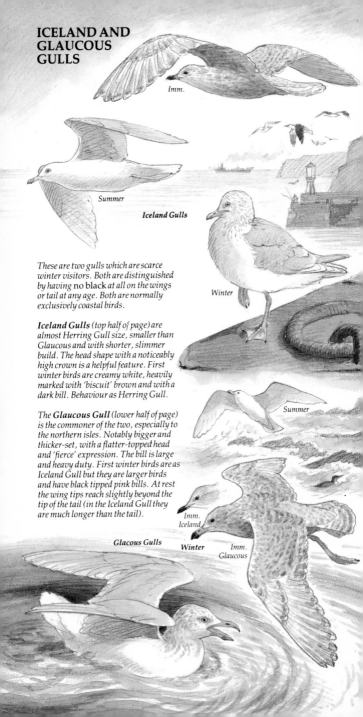

ICELAND AND GLAUCOUS GULLS

Imm.

Summer

Iceland Gulls

Winter

These are two gulls which are scarce winter visitors. Both are distinguished by having *no black* at all on the wings or tail at any age. Both are normally exclusively coastal birds.

Iceland Gulls (*top half of page*) are almost Herring Gull size, smaller than Glaucous and with shorter, slimmer build. The head shape with a noticeably high crown is a helpful feature. First winter birds are creamy white, heavily marked with 'biscuit' brown and with a dark bill. Behaviour as Herring Gull.

The **Glaucous Gull** (*lower half of page*) is the commoner of the two, especially to the northern isles. Notably bigger and thicker-set, with a flatter-topped head and 'fierce' expression. The bill is large and heavy duty. First winter birds are as Iceland Gull but they are larger birds and have black tipped pink bills. At rest the wing tips reach slightly beyond the tip of the tail (in the Iceland Gull they are much longer than the tail).

Summer

Imm. Iceland

Glacous Gulls   **Winter**   *Imm. Glaucous*

SKUAS

Great Skua

Herring Gull

Skuas are dark piratical seabirds which pursue others to force them to disgorge food. Two species are regular round our coasts; two others are rarer.

The **Great Skua** superficially resembles a juvenile gull but is heavier, darker and distinguished by the white wing patches. It has a short tail and broad rounded wings. Often settles on the sea. Regular offshore in spring and autumn; breeds extreme N. Scotland.

Arctic Skua
Light phase

Sandwich Tern

The **Arctic Skua** is the most numerous offshore passage skua, gull-sized with elegant outline and somewhat falcon-like shape. There are pale and dark colour phases, with intermediates. The pale form has a dark cap. Note the pointed central tail feathers. White wing patches vary individually. Piratizes gulls, terns etc. Breeds sparsely in N. and W. Scotland.

Arctic Skua
Dark phase

The rarer **Pomarine Skua** is similar to Arctic but larger and heavier. Note the 'twisted' central tail feathers.

The very rare **Long-tailed Skua** is small and slender with long tail streamers and buoyant graceful flight.

Pomarine Skua

Imm.

Long-tailed Skua

71

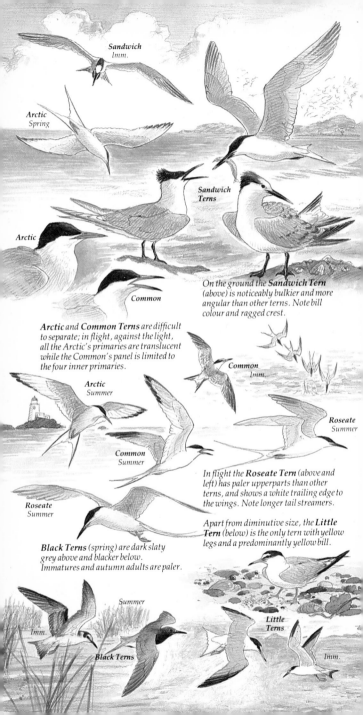

Sandwich *Imm.*

Arctic *Spring*

Sandwich Terns

Arctic

Common

On the ground the **Sandwich Tern** (above) is noticeably bulkier and more angular than other terns. Note bill colour and ragged crest.

Arctic and **Common Terns** are difficult to separate; in flight, against the light, all the Arctic's primaries are translucent while the Common's panel is limited to the four inner primaries.

Common *Imm.*

Arctic *Summer*

Common *Summer*

Roseate *Summer*

Roseate *Summer*

In flight the **Roseate Tern** (above and left) has paler upperparts than other terns, and shows a white trailing edge to the wings. Note longer tail streamers.

Apart from diminutive size, the **Little Tern** (below) is the only tern with yellow legs and a predominantly yellow bill.

Black Terns (spring) are dark slaty grey above and blacker below. Immatures and autumn adults are paler.

Summer

Imm.

Black Terns

Little Terns

Imm.

All our regular sea terns (five species) are white-bodied birds with pale grey wings and black caps. They are all summer visitors nesting on grassy or shingly islands and coastal promontories. They can be tricky to separate by plumage characters at a distance (Common and Arctic particularly so). Offshore, one often has to rely on a combination of voice (Sandwich and Little are very different from the other three) and flight silhouette and flight style. All feed by plunge-diving, often after hovering. In July and August, congregations of mixed species occur on estuaries, sand-bars and other coastal sites.

The **Sandwich Tern** is the earliest arrival of the group (early April, south coasts). The largest British tern, it looks bulkier, shorter-tailed and less agile than the more graceful smaller terns. No tail streamers. Paler grey than others (except Roseate, but this has long streamers and is pure white beneath). The call is distinctive and almost bisyllabic: a harsh grating *"kri-ik"*. Flight is powerful and purposeful with deep wing beats: stiffer and less buoyant than other terns.

The **Common Tern** and **Arctic Tern** are very alike in form, habit and habitat although some Common Terns breed inland on gravel pits and are the only species to do so. On the ground the differences are easier to see. The Common Tern is longer-legged and tends to have a cleaner distinction between the pale underparts and the grey wings and upperparts; the Arctic Tern has a deeper grey belly but clean white throat. Its bill is blood red whereas the Common Tern's is orange-red with a black tip. By autumn, adults of both species have white foreheads (like the immatures) but retain their black caps. Both birds are noisy and have high-pitched chattering *"kee-arr"* calls, which are virtually indistinguishable. Skilled observers identify other fine differences, including the Common Tern's slightly larger bill, dusky trailing edge to underside of primaries, 'neater' plunge and less rapid hovering. Common Terns show a dark wedge on the primaries on the upper wing – a good feature which never occurs on Arctics.

The **Roseate Tern** is superficially very similar to the previous two species but has longer tail streamers, projecting well beyond the wing tips when at rest. It is much paler than either Common or Arctic, with an all-black bill (but with a red base during the breeding season). In flight it is more hurried and short-winged. The pink flush on the breast is an insignificant field character. The alarm call is a drawn out *"kraak"*, sharper and harder than the Common or Arctic. Now a very scarce breeding bird.

The **Little Tern** is much the smallest tern, readily identified by its small size, white forehead, jerky flight with rapid wing beats and trilling, chattering *"kri, kri, kri..."* call. Noisy parties frequently chase above the breeding colony. Little Terns hover more repeatedly and for longer than other terns before plunging.

Of the 'marsh terns' (i.e. freshwater terns) only the **Black Tern** occurs regularly in Britain, usually on passage in May and again in Aug-Sept., mainly in coastal counties of S. and E. England. Feeding birds fly back and forth repeatedly over the water picking insects off the surface.

Summer auks:
Razorbill *(1a-d);*
Guillemot *(2a-c, and bridled form 2d);*
Puffin *(3a,b);* **Black Guillemot** *(4a-c).*

Winter auks: **Razorbill** *(1e,f);*
Guillemot *(2e);* **Puffin** *(3c);* **Black Guillemot** *(4d but compare Velvet Scoter 6);* and **Little Auk** *(5). Beware confusion between winter auks, grebes (7) and divers (8).*

AUKS IN SPRING AND SUMMER. There are five British members of the auk family, all with black (or blackish) upperparts and white underparts. They fly on small whirring wings and legs set far back on the body. Sexes are alike in all species.

In spring and summer, **Guillemots** come to land to nest in dense throngs on the ledges of high sea-cliff colonies scattered all round our coasts and offshore islands (but few east England and the south coast). They fly in and out of the cliffs with fast whirring wings and frequently sit on the sea at the cliff base.

The **Razorbill** is the same size as the Guillemot but can be separated by its black (not dark brown) upperparts and the deep blade-shaped bill. On the sea, the Razorbills sit a little higher in the water and the tail is usually more cocked than the Guillemot's.

The **Black Guillemot** lives close in-shore all the year and is much less communal than the Guillemot and Razorbill. Pairs inhabit rocky, boulder strewn shores, estuaries and inlets in north-west Britain, south to Anglesey: commonest in Scotland and Ireland. Summer plumage is unmistakable. On-shore, breeding birds (and young within boulder-nest sites) produce an annoyingly persistent shrill and reedy whistle "*peeeeeee*", often difficult to locate.

The adult **Puffin** is unmistakable. At sea, the unique tri-coloured bill is still obvious at considerable distances. Otherwise the Puffin is a smaller bird than the Guillemot and Razorbill and in flight is proportionately longer-winged and its orange feet are frequently visible. Puffins breed on offshore islands and lonely cliff slopes off the western and northern seaboards.

AUKS OUTSIDE BREEDING PLUMAGE. From July onwards the auks resort to the open sea to moult into winter plumage and both immatures and adults pose greater problems of identification.

In addition to the difference in bill shape, the **Guillemot's** slimmer build and browner upper plumage still help to distinguish it from the **Razorbill**, (although young Razorbills do not have the adults' deep bill). Note also the white cheek of the Guillemot and the thin dark line running back from the eye. Beware the superficial similarity to winter divers and grebes (see pp. 16-17).

The **Black Guillemot** remains near its breeding site through the autumn and winter. It loses its jet black breeding dress and becomes the palest of all winter auks (beware distant confusion with small winter grebes). Immature birds are similar to winter adults but a little duskier. The bold white wing patch remains.

After breeding, the adult **Puffins** lose part of the grotesque bill and the white face becomes dark grey. Young Puffins are rather similar to winter adults but note the thinner bill. They are usually far out to sea in winter.

The **Little Auk**, which breeds in the high Arctic, occurs sparingly off British coasts in autumn and winter. These are extremely small auks (20cm/8") but despite this they are easy prey for misidentification, often because distances at sea make size-definition difficult. They have extremely small, stubby bills, and a stumpy 'neckless' silhouette. Confusion most frequently occurs with young Puffins but can also include other winter auks.

Woodpigeon

Stock Doves

Woodpigeon (above): a loud wing clapping often accompanies take-off. Note white wing flashes and black bar on fanned tail.

Although plain at first sight, the **Stock Dove's** plumage (above) is in fact a very beautiful mixture of greys, vinous pink, glossy green and black. Note pale grey centre to upper wing.

Rock Dove

Feral Pigeons

Rock Doves (above) rise with a clatter of wings, fly fast and show white underwings as well as a white rump and black wing bars.

The sandy-brown body, black half-collar and tail pattern distinguish the **Collared Dove** (below).

The **Turtle Dove's** graduated white-bordered tail and white belly (below) tell it in flight from Collared Dove.

Collared Doves

Turtle Doves

PIGEONS AND DOVES

The **Woodpigeon** is a heavy-looking, deep-chested bird, familiar as one of our commonest countryside and urban birds. It is easily distinguished by the white neck patches and large white crescents on the upper wing as it flies. Immature birds have no white neck patches.. The cooing call is a variable three to five phrased *"coo-cooo-cooo-cu-cu"* and so on. Big flocks occur in autumn and winter. Although persecution has made rural birds extremely wary, urban ones live in close proximity to man and can be approached easily.

Similar to the Woodpigeon but less numerous is the hole-nesting **Stock Dove**. It is a neater, better-proportioned bird which shows no white at all on its plumage and has no obvious distinguishing features on its blue-grey and dark plumage. Its wing beats are faster than a woodpigeon and it has a distinctly short tail and two abbreviated black wing bars (not broad and distinctive like the Rock Dove). The centre of the wing is very pale grey – a useful identifying character. Stock Doves may occasionally be mistaken for feral pigeons, some of which are similar, so care is needed. It associates freely with feeding flocks of Woodpigeons but rarely occurs in large numbers. The breeding call is a very soft, non-penetrative *"ooo-ooo, ooo-ooo"*.

Wild **Rock Dove** are now confined to remote coasts of western Scotland and Ireland. The true Rock Dove has a white rump patch, black terminal tail band and two conspicuous black bars on the rear part of the inner wing. Many **Feral Pigeons** in town, countryside and along cliff coasts also show these characters. Feral pigeons derive from the original Rock Doves but now have a wide range of plumage based on black, blue and grey, white and cinnamon.

The **Turtle Dove** is a summer migrant commonest in the drier S. and E. and becoming scarce in northern England and beyond the Welsh Marches; it inhabits farmland, copses, woodland edge and railway banks. It is a delicately built and graceful bird, flying agilely with quick bursts of flicking wing beats. This flight pattern is shared with the Collared Dove which distinguishes the two in flight from any other British birds. Both also fly with swept-back wings, unlike other pigeons. The Turtle Dove has a darker appearance in flight due to checkered upperparts and dark tail and primaries. The Turtle Dove's soft purring song is one of the languid sounds of hot summer days.

The sandy-brown plumage of the **Collared Dove** is unlike that of any other British member of the family. It is relieved only by the narrow black half-collar and darker brown flight feathers. The tail pattern is important for separation in flight from the Turtle Dove. From above it is dusky brown and pale tipped; below it is black at the basal end and broadly white on the outer half. The somewhat jerky, uneven flight is characteristic (see Turtle Dove above). The Collared Dove's call, *"coo-coooo-cu"* has the accent on the middle syllable and the third one clipped. It can be interminably persistent and monotonous especially in the early mornings. Collared Doves are now fairly common throughout the country except in mountain areas. They associate closely with human habitations especially when there is ready access to spilled grain – as at farms, flour mills and docks.

Tawny Owls can look surprisingly pale when caught in car headlights (above).

Tawny Owl

Tawny Owls (above) can be located at daytime roost either by careful searching or by following the alarm calls of other birds. Owlets leave the nest long before they can fly and are fed at night by the adults.

The perched silhouette of the **Long-eared Owl** (left) is unmistakable – slim, elongated and often with tufts showing. They use conifer woodland freely and breed in the disused stick nests of other species (below).

Long-eared Owl: although normally nocturnal, autumn migrants may be seen hunting during daytime.

Long-eared Owl

The familiar **Tawny Owl** is numerous (absent Ireland) wherever trees or woodlands offer shelter and nesting sites. It has a large round head and facial disc with big dark eyes. Its 'brown owl' shape and colouring are well known as is its quavering hooting during the breeding season: a di- or tri-syllabic *"hoo-hoo"* is followed by a pause, a short faint *"hoo"* and then drawn out tremulous *"hooo-oo-oo-oo"*. Outside the breeding season the call is a sharp, abbreviated *"ke-wick"*, distinctive and diagnostic (but beware Jays imitating during the daytime!). The perched position is inevitably hunched and the black eyes and dark facial disc give a 'friendly' expression. Often 'sleepy-eyed' when disturbed at roost. Fairly strictly nocturnal, Tawny Owls fly agilely through woodland on broad rounded wings and have separated primaries on the wing tips. They are most easily seen at dusk and dawn when leaving or returning to roost.

There is great similarity, in flight, between the **Long-eared Owl** and closely related Short-eared Owl (see next page). It occupies a wide range of tree habitats from large woods to small stands of trees and is often found in much smaller blocks than Tawny Owl, e.g. small conifer stands, shelter belts. Although usually regarded as strictly nocturnal this species hunts open ground and does occasionally overlap with the daytime Short-eared Owl, particularly from autumn when wintering birds are arriving on this side of the North Sea. The Long-eared Owl's upperparts appear generally darker and more uniform, so much so that the dark 'carpal' patch only shows poorly on the upper wing. Also on the upper wing the primary patch is a rich buff colour compared with the very pale – almost whitish – patch on the Short-eared Owl's wing. The barring on the hind part of the wing is much finer and less distinct than bold barring of Short-eared Owl. It flies with slow wing beats and glides with the wings straight and level (Short-eared Owl's wings appear to be held forward and are in a shallow V). When perched (communal tree roosts occur in winter) there is little likelihood of confusion. The Long-eared Owl has a slim, elongated silhouette with 'ear' tufts regularly erect, and flame orange eyes.

Flight profile of Short-eared Owl (left) compared with Long-eared Owl (right).

Nightjars (see below and pp.84-85), active at dusk and dark plumaged, may be briefly confused with owl species but the long, rather pointed wings, long tail and twisted flight path should quickly identify them.

Male **Snowy Owls** (above) are white with varied spotting and barring: females (right) more heavily barred.

♂

♀

In **short-eared Owl** (below), pale primary wing patches, pale belly and barring on tail are all more obvious than on Long-eared.

Short-eared Owl

When perched on fence post, dune etc., the **Short-eared Owl** (above) shows a heavy-headed appearance and lemon yellow eyes.

Barn Owls (below) hunt with slow flight and dangling feet. They are the only owl with pure white underwings.

Little Owls (bottom) perch on fence posts, old trees etc. and bob and twist ridiculously when agitated or curious. Flight is low-level and markedly undulating.

Barn Owl hunting

Little Owl

OWLS OF DAYTIME AND DUSK

The ghostly image of a hunting **Barn Owl** along roadside or rough field in the gathering dusk is, sadly, an increasingly rare sight. When perched, its white face and underparts, beautiful speckled golden upper-parts and 'knock-kneed' stance are unmistakable. Its rounded head looks disproportionately large and it has dark eyes and a heart-shaped facial disk. Barn Owls are often picked out along roadsides in the headlights of cars and then appear ghostly white, but Tawny Owls too – caught fleetingly in the car's beam – can look very pale. Occasionally a Barn Owl will hunt by day, especially when feeding young, but habitually from early dusk onwards over rough meadows and marshland. They are closely associated with old buildings for nesting, but also use hollow trees. Barn Owls have a spine-chilling, shrieking call and at the nest produce a range of hissing and snoring noises – quite unbirdlike.

The very large all-white **Snowy Owl** breeds in the Arctic and is a winter vagrant to Britain except in the northern isles where a few still occur regularly (it bred in Shetland until recent years). The Snowy Owl is a daytime hunter.

The **Short-eared Owl** is also a daytime hunter. It breeds on moorland, in young conifer plantations and dune systems, mainly in the northern half of the country, and occurs more widely on sand dunes, coastal marshes and downland in winter. It looks pale and could initially be mistaken for a Barn Owl, although principal confusion lies with the Long-eared Owl (see previous page). It has extremely long wings and distinctive low speed, swaying flight (without the Barn Owl's dangling feet); steady, rigid wing beats alternate with wavering glides, and with frequent turning, side-slipping and dipping out of sight to rise again and continue. Its wing tips are rounded, not fingered and the wings have a whitish trailing edge which the Long-eared Owl does not have. Underparts are considerably paler than in the Long-eared Owl (see pp.78-79 for other differences).

The **Little Owl** is by far the smallest of our owls, no bigger than a Song Thrush, and its rotund shape, boldly spotted upperparts, voice and flight make it easy to distinguish. It is regularly abroad in daylight and, when perched, its squat form, longish legs, brilliant lemon eyes and flat-headed, 'frowning', appearance are unique amongst British owls. It is most frequently seen perched on tele-graph poles, fence posts, rocks and the like. When agitated or suspicious it twists its body, bobs and bows in an almost demented manner and can turn its head easily through 180 degrees to look around it. It flies fast and low with rapid wings in bounding undulations. Its principal call is a shrill *"kiew, kiew"*. Although widely distributed in England and parts of Wales, the Little Owl prefers lowland agricultural areas with old hedgerows, trees and parkland. It is very rare in Scotland, and absent from Ireland.

Short-eared Owl, hunting flight.

Swifts

Swallows

♀

♂

Silhouette and speed of flight normally identify **Swifts** (above) easily. They have dusky plumage, pale chin (seldom seen), a neckless appearance and short forked tail.

Imm.

Immature **Swallows** (above) have a V-shaped tail and no streamers. They nest in outbuildings (below). **House Martins'** (right) build mud nests under eaves.

The male **Swallow** (above) has longer tail-streamers than the female. From below, the Swallow shows chestnut throat and a dark chest band.

House Martin

Sand Martins (left and below) have earth-brown upperparts and a brown chest band on white underparts.

House Martin

SWALLOWS AND SWIFT

The **Swift** is distinguished from all other birds by its flight silhouette – long, narrow, scythe-shaped wings – its sooty black plumage and the speed of its flight. Arriving from early May onwards, screaming parties of Swifts soon chase noisily through the airspace above most of our towns and villages. They are exclusively aerial, roosting, feeding and even mating on the wing and only 'landing' when entering their nest-holes under the eaves of buildings. They are the fastest of all birds in level flight and are unlikely to be confused with any others. They feed high in the sky in warm dry weather, but hunt almost at ground level over meadows, parks and playing fields when rainy weather grounds their insect prey. Most have left again by late August.

The **Swallow** is relatively easily identified from the martins (see below) by its relaxed, sweeping and graceful flight, metallic blue upperparts, pale underparts and long tail-streamers. In fresh spring plumage, the male's streamers are noticeably longer then the female's but abrasion and damage through the summer often confuses the difference. Young Swallows have deeply forked tails but no streamers. In autumn, large numbers congregate on wires, often in company with House Martins; otherwise they are not particularly communal, except at roosts (reed-beds) on autumn passage. Swallows have a pleasant twittering song, usually when perched. Parties of Swallows will often noisily pursue birds of prey – Kestrel, Sparrowhawk – or Cuckoos and thereby draw attention to them. Individuals return to the same site each year, nesting in barns and outbuildings.

House Martins nest communally under the eaves of buildings, occasionally bridges and even cliffs, constructing enclosed nests of mud, often one against another. Their bodies are wholly white underneath (compare Sand Martin) and glossy blue-black above; the colouring on the head forms a mask-like facial pattern which makes the eyes 'invisible'. The most important character, however, is the pure white rump which immediately separates the House Martin from other hirundines. Young birds, and adults towards the end of the season, appear browner above and lack much of the blue gloss. The birds produce a pianissimo twittering song, both perched and on the wing, and also twitter from nests at dawn. They are more gregarious than Swallows. When nest building, the birds can be seen landing on the ground to collect soft mud from farmyards, puddles and stream-sides: this is normally the only time they land.

House Martin and **Sand Martin** are similar in flight silhouette (but House Martin glides more regularly), but as long as good light allows colours and patterns to be seen, there should be no problem of identification. The Sand Martin is the smallest of the European swallows, with earth-brown upperparts and a dark chest band across its otherwise white underparts (compare House Martin). It is among the earliest of spring arrivals, from early March onwards, and has a fast, flitting flight with relatively little gliding. Nesting colonies are in soft banks, often river sides or sand pits, collections of flattened holes indicating their presence. They congregate in large reed-bed roosts on spring and autumn passage.

Cuckoo

Rufous phase

Nightjar

♂

Imm.

The **Nightjar** has an elongated
appearance and grey-brown plumage to
give perfect camouflage. The broad head
has a very small bill but wide gape for
catching moths.

When perched (top), drooping wings
cover the **Cuckoo's** patterned
underparts. Young birds (above) are
grey brown or brown. All have a white
patch at back of head.

♂

♀

The green-and-black female
Golden Oriole (above right) can be
confused with Green Woodpecker.

The **Hoopoe's** black-and-white
patterned wings and tail are unlike any
other British bird. In flight it brings to
mind a huge butterfly.

♂

♀

The female **Kingfisher** has a red lower
mandible distinguishing her from the
male with all-black bill.

CUCKOO, NIGHTJAR, GOLDEN ORIOLE, KINGFISHER, HOOPOE

The male **Cuckoo's** song needs no introduction – the best-known of all bird calls. The bird itself is less familiar and can be difficult to find as individuals are intentionally inconspicuous. Much of their travel around the breeding area is so low-level – along ditches and hedges – as to be below our normal sight line. In open flight, the Cuckoo is long-tailed, pointed-winged and has a distinctly hawk-like outline (but Sparrowhawk has rounded wings; see pp. 44-45). It flies without wings rising above horizontal. Sexes are alike; the presence of brownish feathers on the female's 'bib' sometimes helps but is not reliable. Some females appear distinctly small. Cuckoos inhabit a wide range of countryside habitats; females return to the same areas each year, to the same host species as that by which they were reared, usually Dunnock, Meadow Pipit or Reed Warbler, depending on habitat.

The crepuscular **Nightjar** is a decreasing species of heathland, bracken hillsides and young plantations mainly in southern Britain. Hidden during the day, the Nightjar emerges at dusk to hunt for insects on the wing. Its flight, on long narrow wings, is twisting and erratic, silent and ghostly like a huge fast-flying moth. The female's plumage is unrelieved but the male has white spots at the base of the outer primaries and white tips to the outer tail feathers. As well as crouching camouflaged on the ground during the day, birds will also 'lie' horizontally along tree branches. Nightjars are probably best known for the remarkable nocturnal churring song of the male – very protracted and resembling the sound of a two-stroke engine, rising and falling in the distance.

The male **Golden Oriole's** plumage is unique and unmistakable. A few birds occur on spring and autumn passage and the species breeds sparingly in S.E. England. Despite the brilliance of the male – and to a lesser degree the female – the birds are very shy and occupy deep foliage, often high in the tree-tops and are therefore not necessarily easy to see. The male's song is a loud melodious whistling, distinctive and unmistakable once heard. Females can be confused with Green Woodpecker (pp. 86-87).

The **Kingfisher** is the most brilliantly coloured of all British birds and cannot be confused with any other. It is fairly common on slow-moving rivers where soft banks provide opportunities for excavating nesting tunnels. Despite its brilliance, it can be located far more readily if the call is known; a shrill, piercing *"chee"* as the bird flies very rapidly above the watercourse. When seen, it is most often as a blue streak flying away up-river. Patience or luck is required to get good views of a Kingfisher. Young birds are less brilliant, have shorter bills and dark legs and feet. Kingfishers are few in Scotland but well distributed elsewhere, particularly in the lowlands. Numbers are seriously affected by severe winters.

Each spring some **Hoopoes** 'overshoot' their European breeding areas and arrive in Britain – perhaps 100 a year. Understandably, the greatest numbers are seen in S. coast counties in March-May. Very occasionally a pair attempts to breed. Hoopoes are unmistakable birds which obligingly hunt for insect food on open ground such as lawns and parks. Salmon-pink plumage and long crest – either raised or lowered – identify the Hoopoe immediately.

Green Woodpecker

Great Spotted ♂

Imm.

Imm.

♀

♀

♂

Lesser Spotted

♂

Nuthatch

Green Woodpecker: *our only large green bird. The green plumage, bright crimson crown and striking yellow rump are unmistakable. Immatures have red crowns and streaky underparts.*

The **Lesser Spotted Woodpecker** (below) *is a very small and elusive bird. The finely barred back and nearly all-white underparts are diagnostic.*

The male **Great Spotted Woodpecker** (above) *has a scarlet nape; immatures have the whole crown crimson. Separated from Lesser Spotted by larger size, white 'shoulder' patches and crimson under tail.*

The **Nuthatch's** *facial pattern (below) is distinctive. The colour of underparts is buffish but the male's flanks are usually a more strongly marked rusty colour than the female's.*

The **Wryneck** (above) *is a scarce migrant, mainly found on the E. coast. Head feathers are raised when the bird is excited or agitated.*

WOODPECKERS, WRYNECK, NUTHATCH

The **Green Woodpecker** is unlikely to be confused with any other species. It is the largest of our woodpeckers, with green plumage, a prominent yellowish rump and strong bill. This bird is less arboreal than other woodpeckers, finding much food (particularly ants) on the ground, where it alternately probes in the ground and raises its head to look around for danger. It moves around with somewhat ungainly hops. The flight is deeply undulating with wings closed each time it dips down. The male has a crimson centre to its moustachial stripe, lacking in the female. Young birds have black streaked faces and mottled underparts. The Green Woodpecker's call is a well-known laughing yaffle which is far-carrying. It seldom drums. Absent from Ireland.

Although it is brightly coloured, the **Great Spotted Woodpecker** is not necessarily the easiest of birds to see. The hard metallic *"chik"* call is often the best way to locate it. It is a woodland bird, emerging to gardens in winter when it will frequent bird tables. The strident drumming (Feb.-May) comprises a sequence of 10-15 lightning-quick hammer blows lasting less than a second, frequently repeated. This drumming is at its most characteristic when done on resonant dead branches. In flight, four or five wing beats alternate with complete wing closures to give a strongly undulating flight. The male has a crimson nape patch, absent in the female. This woodpecker climbs up trees with quick staccato jerks, each individual movement very rapid. Absent from Ireland.

The tiny **Lesser Spotted Woodpecker** is only slightly larger than the Nuthatch (see below). It is often elusive and spends a lot of its time in the highest branches and twigs as well as working the main body of trees. It displays some partiality for damp areas where it is often associated with alders, willows and similar easily worked wood. It also frequents old orchards, gardens, urban parks as well as open woodland. Absent from Scotland and Ireland. It is usually most readily located by the clear penetrating *"pee, pee, pee..."* call. It has no red on undersides but the male has a dullish crimson crown. The 'drumming' is often performed high up in trees, and is much softer, less far-carrying but more protracted than the Great Spotted.

The **Wryneck**, formerly widespread, is now only seen as a scarce spring and, especially, autumn migrant. It is a somewhat undistinguished bird, cryptically coloured with mottled brown and grey plumage (similar colouring to Nightjar). Migratory, it is in almost all respects unlike other members of the woodpecker family and more reminiscent of passerines. It is most frequently seen at coastal migration points. It flies in a sluggish, undulating manner and, when perched, has a sinuous, reptilian mien.

The **Nuthatch** is a common woodland and garden bird in southern Britain (rare north of Yorkshire-Lancashire and absent from Ireland). It is our only blue-grey arboreal bird, with whitish underparts. Climbs both upwards and downwards on trees with equal facility – the only bird to do so. Territorial throughout the year and therefore calls at all seasons – a piercing *"piu, piu, piu..."* and a trilling *"chi-chi-chi..."*. In habit and behaviour it has many of the characteristics of a small woodpecker.

Skylark

Skylark Imm.

In its song flight, the **Skylark** (above) is unmistakable. This flight is almost vertical, both in ascent and descent, often taking the bird to great height where it remains hovering or hanging, head to wind. Final stage of descent is an abrupt drop to the ground.

Note the **Woodlark's** (right) white eye-stripe, meeting at back of head, short dark tail and the erectile crest. Woodlarks perch much more freely than skylarks and appear very short and stubby.

Woodlark

Skylark

The uniform upperparts and striking face pattern make the **Shore Lark** (left) readily identifiable. In spring the head pattern becomes much stronger. The male has a black crown band and tiny 'horns' (below).

Shore Lark

Lark

Pipit

The familiar **Skylark**, with its cascading aerial song, is a bird of open grassy places ranging from larger fields on farmland to sand dunes, moorland, downland and salt marshes. It is the most widespread of all British breeding birds and very numerous in some areas. The Skylark is a brown bird, strongly streaked with black above and with white underparts and streaked breast. The tail is blackish with white outer feathers and the wings have a whitish trailing edge. The slightly tufted crest is raised when the bird is agitated, excited or nervous, at which times it often stands in a tall upright stance. In sustained flight, it flies in long, even undulations, closing the wings at times as it drives forward. The frequent contact call is a lively *"chirr-up"*. Large flocks on arable land and coastal marshes in winter include many continental birds.

The **Woodlark** is a rare and declining species in Britain, now only found in a handful of southern counties. It inhabits dry areas of heath, grassland and downs, where there are also available trees for song posts; it is also found in plantation clearings (East Anglia) and areas of felled woodland. It is a 'typical' lark with brown, streaked plumage and a more rounded crest than the Skylark, which is not usually raised however. Its tail is very short and lacks white outer feathers. At short range, a small dark mark near the bend of the wing can be seen and is diagnostic. The beautiful song consists of a short (three- to five-second) sequence of liquid, fluty notes *"lu-lu-lu-lu…"* on a strongly descending scale. It is delivered from a song perch on bush or tree, or during a wide spiralling song flight, and it not infrequently sings at night. It feeds unobtrusively on the ground, where it also roosts, but it perches much more freely than other larks.

The rather scarce winter-visiting **Shore Lark** is a plain grey-brown bird with pale underparts, but is easily distinguished by the strong facial pattern. Birds are seldom visible unless flushed, although feeding groups may betray their presence by a double call-note *"see-seoo"*. Between October and March, these Shore Larks from Scandinavia feed in small numbers on coastal marshes, shingles and adjacent grasslands in E. England, sometimes associating with Skylark flocks. Occasional pairs breed in the Scottish Highlands.

Woodlark, display flight

Meadow Pipit

Meadow Pipit (left and above):
the black streaking on the breast forms a
small dense patch in the centre. Mainly
terrestrial, they perch most often when
taking food to young in the nest.

Song flight

Tree Pipit

Tree Pipit (above): in spring, the
parachuting song flight is unmistakable.
Note paler legs, slightly stockier form
and yellower breast than Meadow Pipit.

Rock Pipit (left) is larger and darker
than other pipits. It has pale eye-ring
and supercilium and very dark legs.
Water Pipit (below) has white outer
tail feathers (not smoky as in Rock), dark
legs, whitish supercilium: winter only.

Rock Pipit

Water Pipit

Three species breed and one sub-species occurs as a winter visitor. Several other species occur as rare autumn vagrants. Pipits are small brown birds with streaky plumage and whitish outer tail feathers; mainly terrestrial, they run or walk briskly and jerkily. Beware confusion with larks (pp. 88-89) on the ground: pipits tend to use their tails, wagtail-like, which larks do not. Pipits can be extremely confusing and are most safely identified by a combination of voice, plumage, habits and habitats rather than simply by plumage; **Meadow Pipit** and **Tree Pipit** are particularly difficult. The Meadow Pipit is an extremely numerous species in summer, in open country from sea level to mountain tops. The Tree Pipit is a widely distributed summer visitor to mainland Britain but oddly absent from Ireland. The main differences are summarized below.

Meadow Pipit	Tree Pipit
Open uplands and uncultivated lowlands (summer); lowland pastures and coastal marshes in loose flocks (winter).	Parkland, woodland edge and shrubby hillsides. Summer visitor only.
Slightly more olive-brown upperparts; breast whiter and heavily streaked; legs pale brown.	Upper parts warmer brown; yellower/buffer background to breast; pale flesh-coloured legs.
Mainly terrestrial, but perches on fence posts, wires etc., especially when feeding young.	Usually perches on outer sprays of bushes, trees etc.
Song flight to and from ground.	Song flight from one tree perch to another.

Winter flocks of Meadow Pipits rise and fly a few at a time, not as one flock as Starlings etc. do. The Meadow Pipit has a fluttering upward song flight with gliding descent and a thin piping song increasing in pace and terminating on descent with a short trill. The call is thin, shrill *"tseep"* or *"tseep, tseep"*. The Tree Pipit's lovely parachuting song flight is accompanied by a superior and more musical song, far-carrying, with a distinctive terminal *"cheea, cheea, cheea..."*. The call is a distinct, slightly rasping *"pizzz"*. Tree Pipits have a characteristic 'pumping' action of the tail as they walk. Both species have whiter outer tail feathers.

The darker and slightly larger **Rock Pipit** aids identification by its extremely restricted habitat requirement; it is a littoral bird almost wholly confined to rocky coasts between tideline and clifftop, where it favours sheltered gullies, geos and inlets. It forages amongst the tide wrack, rocks and boulders where its dark plumage makes it difficult to pick out until it moves. It is not only larger than our other common pipits but has a longer bill which gives it a more elongated appearance. Outer feathers are smoky white and legs dark (compare other pipits). It has a song flight similar to Meadow Pipit and a characteristic *"phist"* call note.

The **Water Pipit** and the Rock Pipit are in fact the same species, being simply distinct races. Water Pipits breed in the mountains of Europe and small numbers winter in the southern half of Britain on sewage farms, watercress beds, estuaries and coastal marshes.

Imm.

Grey Wagtails ♂

♀

Yellow Wagtails ♀

At all seasons the **Grey Wagtail** (above) has a long black tail with white outer feathers, constantly wagged. Note yellow rump. Male loses black bib at end of breeding season.

♂

Imm.

Blue-headed ♂

Male **Yellow Wagtails** (above) vary in the intensity of their colour; the above is a strongly marked individual. Female is duller above and much paler below.

The **White Wagtail** only occurs in spring and autumn and has a pale grey mantle and rump, not black as in Pied Wagtail.

Pied Wagtail (below): both sexes lose the black throat in winter, but retain a broad black breast band. In autumn, immature Pied and White Wagtails are indistinguishable.

♂

Pied Wagtails

Imm.

Winter

White Wagtail

The **Grey Wagtail** is a waterside bird found on fast-flowing, bouldery streams often in the same places as Dippers (pp.94-95). Accordingly, it is particularly associated with hill country and is most numerous in the N. and W. of Britain (but absent from northern isles and Outer Hebrides). In winter it occurs more widely in the lowlands but always closely associated with water habitats, although often seen in towns at that time of year too. Both sexes are grey above and bright canary-yellow below; in spring the male is distinguished by having a bold black bib. In winter both sexes have white throats and buffish breasts. The Grey Wagtail has a very long tail which is constantly wagged. It searches for insects on stream-side shingles and boulders, often pursuing flying ones in lively dancing aerial excursions. Its normal flight is in a series of deep undulations. The flight call is a sharp metallic *"siz-eet"* – more bi-syllabic than the Pied Wagtail's.

Although individual males vary in the intensity of their plumage, there is little likelihood of confusing the **Yellow Wagtail**. It is a summer visitor to water meadows, damp pastures and coastal marshes; it occurs restrictedly in Wales, southwest England and lowland Scotland and does not normally reach Ireland. Yellow Wagtails feed actively on the ground with brisk gait, darting action and backward and forward motion of the head as they walk or run. They are often in cattle-grazed pastures. The male has a brilliant canary-yellow head and underparts with slightly greener upperparts. The females are considerably duller birds with browner upperparts and paler yellow underparts. Young birds are more pipit-like in appearance, greyish-brown above and buff below with distinct breast markings. The all-yellow male is restricted to Britain and males of the continental race have blue heads (females are the same as our birds) and are sometimes found among our breeding populations, particularly in the south-east. Yellow wagtails fly with dipping, undulating flight and have a very distinctive *"sweep"* call. After the breeding season, passage birds appear at sewage farms, riversides and reservoir edges.

The **Pied Wagtail** is a common urban and rural bird, not confined to the water's edge, but often found in towns, gardens, roadsides, quarries or farms. Although a strongly patterned black and white bird which is fairly readily identified, the plumage variations – both seasonal and sexual – are confusing within the species – a confusion added to by the White Wagtail (see below). The spring-plumaged male has black back, throat and tail, white cheeks and forehead and grey flanks; in winter the back is much greyer. Spring females have dark grey backs and less black on the head and breast. Pied Wagtails hunt for insects on short turf or the water's edge, marching with deliberate gait and frequent darting runs. They often make brief aerial sallies to catch insects disturbed from the grass. The call is a hard *"chis-ick"*.

The **White Wagtail** is the same species as Pied Wagtail, and is the continental breeding race which occurs in Britain only on spring (April-May) and autumn passage (Aug.-Oct.). The birds have pale grey mantle and rump – the Pied Wagtail's rump is black in all plumages. Behaviour, habitat and calls are as Pied Wagtail.

Waxwings

Great Grey Shrike

The **Waxwing's** pinkish-brown crest, short yellow-tipped tail and bold face pattern are unmistakable. At close range, note the white marks on wing and red waxy tips to secondary feathers. First winter birds lack white in wings.

The bold black, white and grey patterning make the **Great Grey Shrike** (above) easy to identify.

Red-backed Shrike

♀

♂

Red-backed Shrike (above): male's patterned head and tail contrast with the rich chestnut back and closed wings. Females lack the black 'mask' and tail, which is bright chestnut; note 'scaly' underparts.

The **Tree Creeper** (left) moves mouse-like up the trunks of trees.

The tiny, stubby **Wren** (below) has a distinctive shape and loud vehement song.

Dipper

Wren

WAXWING, SHRIKES, WREN, DIPPER
TREECREEPER

Most winters see visits by **Waxwings** from the forests of northern Europe and occasionally there are considerable influxes. Waxwings resemble tubby Starlings at a distance, both in size and in outline; the similarity ends there, however, as the Waxwing is a brightly coloured bird unlikely to offer confusion with other species. They feed on haws, cotoneaster berries, rowans and other berries in gardens and town parks as well as in the open countryside and are often very approachable. After feeding, birds often sit immobile for a long time. Sexes are alike. When they occur, Waxwings are usually only found in small parties.

The **Great Grey Shrike** is a solitary winter visitor from Scandinavia (Oct. onwards) thinly distributed across the country: individuals often return to the same vicinity each year. It is a predatory bird which feeds on large insects, small mammals and birds, for which it hunts from exposed perches on wires or bushes. Flight from one perch to another is usually low with a terminal upward glide to the perch. These shrikes are very aggressive, even to birds of prey that pass through their hunting territory.

Formerly widespread, the **Red-backed Shrike** is now a very rare and declining summer visitor, a few pairs breeding in S. and south-east England. They inhabit thickets, overgrown commons, downs and similar areas. Small prey are sometimes impaled on thorns as a 'larder'. In addition to the breeding birds, others occur as drift migrants on the E. coast in autumn and less frequently in spring. Perching and flight characteristics as Great Grey Shrike. Young birds resemble females but have even more scaly crescent markings. Like the Great Grey Shrike, this bird has the hook-tipped bill of the true predator.

The **Wren**, like the Dunnock (see pp. 124-125), operates mainly at or near ground level. Familiar and ubiquitous, its strident song, used all year, is vehement and far-carrying, the most positive of bird songs to be heard through the winter months. The alarm call is a harsh "*tuc, tuc, tuc*". Sexes are alike. Wrens occupy a wider range of habitats – from seashore to mountain-side – than almost any other British species.

The **Dipper** is one of the easiest of British birds to identify. Plump, brown-plumaged, with a tail frequently cocked, it has a striking white throat and breast and inhabits fast-flowing, boulder-strewn streams in the uplands. It feeds in the body of the water, in the main stream, disappearing below the surface to search for caddis and other insect larvae. When perched on rock or boulder it bobs rhythmically. It flies fast and low over the water, slavishly following the course of the stream.

Although the mouse-like movements of the **Tree-creeper** often make it inconspicuous, once it is seen, it is unlikely to be confused with any other. Having worked its way mincingly up one tree, probing the bark for insects, it will fly down again to the base of another tree to start again. It moves up the tree in a jerky spiralling course, probing the crevices of the bark with its thin curved bill. It often roosts in little hollows scraped in the soft bark of welling-tonias a few feet above ground level. It has the thinnest of calls, Goldcrest-like and high pitched, "*tsee*".

Spring ♀

Whinchats

Autumn ♂

Stonechats

♀

Spring ♀

Stonechats *(above) use prominent open perches: dumpy shape and bold colouring are distinctive.*

Whinchat ♂

♂

The **Whinchat** *(above and right) is slenderer than Stonechat. Note the white supercilium and white wing patches on open wing – less prominent on female.*

Imm.

Robin

Nightingale

Imm.

Immature **Robins** *(above) and* **Nightingales** *(below) are alike apart from latter's longer chestnut tail. Nightingales (left) are heard more frequently than seen.*

CHATS, NIGHTINGALE, ROBIN

The resident **Stonechat** is predominantly a bird of rough heather, bracken and gorse brakes in coastal areas; less frequent inland except in Ireland where it is widespread. Its silhouette is slightly plump and it is a pleasantly extrovert and approachable bird, typically perching on topmost twig, fence wire or post. It drops frequently to the ground to feed and then returns to a favourite eminence. It has a dancing, hovering display flight, more relaxed and showy than the somewhat frenetic song flights of Whitethroat or Sedge Warbler. Birds indulge in much tail flirting and wing flicking. The male's distinctive spring plumage becomes browner and duller after the late-summer moult. Young birds and females are duller, with streaked brown upperparts and no white on rump or neck. They can be confused with Whinchat so look for presence or absence of supercilium and more portly shape of Stonechat. The frequent scolding *"shak-shak"* or *"weet, shak-shak"* is aptly likened to the clinking together of two pebbles.

The closely related **Whinchat** is also helpfully conspicuous, always perching on the outside of bushes etc. as prominent song perches. Both species have pleasing jingling songs typical of the short metallic phrases of most chats. The Stonechat's has a Dunnock-like quality but the Whinchat's is the more musical of the two. Whinchats are one of the later summer visitors to arrive (late April and through May). They inhabit open country which provides a combination of rough grassy areas and bushes (old commons, new plantations, rough hillsides, railway banks) and are nowadays much commoner in the hill country of the N. and W. than in lowland England. Distinctly short-tailed in outline they are slenderer and have a less upright stance than Stonechats. The *"tic-tic"* alarm is less hard. A little care is needed to avoid confusion with female or young Stonechats. The most important distinguishing plumage feature is the prominent white supercilium and white moustachial stripe (especially male Whinchat); white base to tail feathers is diagnostic at all times and the white flash on wing (less evident in the female) is also obvious. Sexes are similar, although male is markedly brighter in spring and summer but much more like female in autumn. The female has a smaller wing patch and a buffish eye-stripe. Young birds have no wing patch and are more easily confused with young Stonechats – but remember the white supercilium and tail patches.

The **Nightingale** is more famed – and probably more familiar to birdwatchers – for its song than for its appearance. Alone amongst our commoner chats it is fairly skulking in habit, being a dweller in the undergrowth of deciduous woods, thickets and overgrown hedgerows mainly S. and E. of a line from Humber to Severn. Its song is superb: rich and fluid, the most distinctive part is a slow *"piuu piuu…"* accelerating to a passionate crescendo. It sings chiefly by day but also regularly at night when its magnificence is undiluted by other bird song. Sexes are alike; bright chestnut tail distinguishes it from other birds in the same habitat. The young can be distinguished from the immature **Robins** (which are otherwise very similar) by the same feature. The adult Robin is perhaps the only British bird that is universally recognised.

Black Redstart

Redstart

Redstart
Autumn

*Male **Redstart** (above) is brightly
coloured. The chestnut tail is frequently
bobbed and constantly quivered.*

*Females and immature **Black
Redstarts** (above) resemble
female Redstarts but are
darker and smokier, without
pale buff or whitish throat or
underparts.*

Spring

Wheatear

Autumn   Imm.

Spring

Bluethroat (below): look for chestnut
tail panels as bird flies from one piece of
cover to the next. It constantly flicks and
fans its tail. Throat pattern in autumn is
varied; most males show some blue and
some of the chestnut band.

Wheatear's shape (above) and pattern
are distinctive; note white rump and tail
pattern and erect posture on the ground.

Bluethroat

Autumn   Imm.

REDSTARTS, WHEATEAR, BLUETHROAT

The male **Redstart** is our most colourful common summer visitor with bright plumage and a flashing chestnut tail. It is numerous on passage and a widespread breeding bird in old woodlands, commons, parkland, old buildings or stone walls. It is virtually absent from Ireland, rather scarce in S. and E. England but numerous in hill areas elsewhere. Autumn males lose the brilliance of spring and summer and are less showy. Females are altogether paler birds, a soft grey-brown above and buffish-white below, whitish throat and the same distinctive tail. Immatures are similar to young Robins (see pp. 96-97) but with chestnut tails. The male's song is a brief, almost mechanical jingle of notes – an apparent introduction for a grander song which never occurs. The distinctive alarm is *"wheet-tik-tik"* (same cadence as Stonechat, pp. 88-89); also a liquid *"wheet"* call, similar to those of the Willow Warbler and the Chiff Chaff but a little harder.

Black Redstarts occur mainly as coastal migrants, although small numbers also winter, notably near coasts on cliffs, harbour buildings etc. There is a small breeding population, mainly in the south-eastern quarter of Britain – the only rare British breeding species mainly confined to urban areas. The summer male is matt sooty grey with blacker underparts and, in addition to the obvious rusty tail, adult males have a pale whitish wing patch. However, full adult plumage is not attained until two years old. Autumn and winter males are paler and less well marked. The song is a loud, clear, key-jingling warble, reminiscent of the common Redstart but lacking that musical quality, delivered from high up on a building, television aerial or the like.

The **Wheatear** is a ground-living species, requiring short grazed turf on which to feed and available rabbit burrows etc. in which to nest. Spring arrivals start from mid-March and the species breeds widely but most numerously in the hill country of N. and W. They are restless birds, with much flitting, bobbing and tail fanning, frequently moving from one small eminence to another, flying fast and low to the ground before rising to wall-top, mole hill or boulder. On the ground they move in long hops. Both sexes have an eye-catching white rump and distinctive tail pattern. Female has same pattern as male but with black areas replaced by brown. By autumn, males are already browner and more difficult to separate from females. The call is loud: a hard *"chak"* or *"chak-wheet"* and the song a loose medley of both wheezy and musical notes, short in duration and usually delivered from a low-level song-perch. Some individuals in late May are notably bright and large and belong to the Greenland race.

Modest numbers of **Bluethroats** occur each year, mainly on the E. coast in autumn; a few in spring. The conspicuous rusty panels at the base of the brown tail are the diagnostic feature to look for, otherwise both sexes (autumn) have mid-brown upperparts and are white below. Females have a white throat and speckled chest band. Spring males are unmistakable. It is an extremely skulking bird, especially on passage. Most records are of the red-spotted (Scandinavian) form; the white-spotted (E. European) form is much the rarer in Britain.

Imm.

Blackbirds

♂

♂

♀

Ring Ouzels

Blackbirds *(above): individual females can often be told apart, showing differing degrees of rufous or pinkish on the under-parts. Male's bill does not become full-blooded orange yellow until spring of the year after hatching.*

♀

Song Thrush

Male **Ring-Ouzel** *(above) has clear white gorget. Female is browner with duller, narrower crescent and scaly underparts.*

Redwing

Song Thrush's *(above): the song is distinctive for its continual repetition of phrases.*

Song

Fieldfare *(below right) is identified by slate grey head and rump, rufous back and black tail as well as rusty shading on breast.*

Mistle

Mistle Thrush *(below) is large and pale and has an upright stance.*

Fieldfare

Mistle Thrush

Redwings

Imm.

Fieldfare

The male **Blackbird**, is familiar and unmistakable but some other plumages cause uncertainty. First winter males show much more brown especially on the streaky underparts, flight feathers and coverts. The female is blackish-brown above with a pale grey chin and warm brown underparts variably streaked and blotched blackish. A noisy and excitable bird, with much tail flicking and alarm calling, especially at dusk – *"chink...chink"*. The song is rich and melodious.

Ring Ouzels are summer visitors which arrive from mid-March on S. coast headlands and downs, but they pass on quickly to the hills of Wales, northern England and Scotland. On territory they have a clear ringing song – *"cheroo, cheroo cheri, chi-cho-oo"* – a short sequence of double notes repeated three to four times with pauses between. Usually the only genuine songster to be heard in the wild gullies, ravines and heather banks where it breeds. It also has a piping *"pee-u"* call and a harsh Blackbird-like alarm call; *"shak, shak, shak"*. They can often be located at a considerable distance by their clear song or harsh chattering alarm but they may otherwise be surprisingly difficult to see against the dark backgrounds of the areas where they nest. The male's colour is more sooty-black than the Blackbird's and the pale wing patch is easily visible. Body feathers in autumn have pale edges which give the bird a scaly appearance.

Warm brown upperparts and the strongly spotted underparts of the **Song Thrush** contrast with the **Redwing's** streaked breast, strong head patterning and rich chestnut flanks. In flight distinction between the two is less easy: look for the chestnut underwing of the Redwing and the paler yellower underwing of the Song Thrush. The Song Thrush's loud musical song is distinctive and easily distinguishable from the Blackbird's richer mellow warbling by its characteristic repetition of phrases. Both birds have a distinctive *"sipp"* flight call but the Song Thrush's *"zip"* is the less penetrating and more clipped. On calm nights in autumn, listen for the Redwing's thin *"siip"* contact note overhead as thousands of these Scandinavian night migrants pass over.

The **Mistle Thrush** is the largest of our thrushes, slightly bigger than the superficially similar Fieldfare. It has pale grey-brown upperparts and closely spotted underparts: note diagnostic white tips on outer tail feathers, especially when it fans its tail on landing. An early-season songster, its loud somewhat harsh song is characteristic of wild late-winter days. The alarm call is a harsh rattle.

Both Mistle Thrush and **Fieldfare** show white underwing patches in flight. Both are strong fliers, but the Mistle Thrush's flight is more undulating with prolonged closing of the wings. Fieldfares, like the Redwings with which they regularly consort in flocks, are highly gregarious on farmland in winter, feeding first on hedgerow berries and later on the ground for fallen fruit, invertebrates and seeds. Flocks often betray their presence overhead by the harsh *"chack, chack, chack"* flight call. Often, several thrush species congregate together in large winter roosts in shrubbery or other undergrowth.

Display

Imm.

**Willow
Warbler**

Chiffchaff

Chiffchaff: (above) legs are usually
dark. The bill too is all-dark and the
supercilium less well marked than
Willow Warbler's.
The **Willow Warbler** (top right) is
marginally larger and less dumpy than
Chiffchaff. Plumage appears brighter
and lower mandible is pale orange. Legs
usually pale.

The **Wood Warbler** (below)
sings whilst moving about under
tree canopy, often in sailing,
display flight. Note bright yellow
breast and white belly. Has longer
wings than other leaf warblers.

Goldcrest

♂

Wood Warbler

♀

Firecrest (below): the black-and-white
eye-stripes are the most important
identification feature.

The black-bordered crown of the
Goldcrest (above) is flame-coloured in
the male and yellow in the female, but it
is not always immediately conspicuous.

*Goldcrest
Imm.*

Firecrest

LEAF WARBLERS AND GOLDCRESTS

The **Willow Warbler**, is our most numerous and widespread summer visitor, breeding wherever scattered bushes and trees give a mixture of open ground and low cover. This small slender bird is most readily distinguished from the very similar **Chiffchaff** by its distinctive song – a delicate and refined warbling on a descending scale, one of the familiar sounds of spring, continuing well into the summer. The Chiffchaff's song, *"chiff, chaff, chaff, chiff, chiff, chaff…"*, often delivered from the crown of a tree is unmistakable. Both birds have a soft *"hweet"* call, the Chiffchaff's being clearly monosyllabic and the Willow Warbler's more drawn out, *"hooweet"* (see also Redstart, pp. 98-99). The Chiffchaff is a drabber bird, considerably the more thinly distributed of the two and mainly confined to well wooded areas which also offer rough undergrowth for nesting. It is markedly scarce in northern Scotland. Juveniles of both species have yellower underparts than their respective adults.

The **Wood Warbler** is distinctly larger and more cleanly coloured than the other two leaf warblers. Its upperparts are greener, throat and breast more definitely yellowish and the underparts pure white; its bright yellow supercilium is easily noticeable. Wood Warblers live in deciduous woodlands and are especially numerous in the old sessile woods of N. and W. Britain, where grazing keeps ground cover to a minimum. The male Wood Warbler has two distinct songs, both of which it uses while moving about in the tree canopy or flying from one song branch to another, the whole body shivering as it delivers the song. Its best known song begins as a modulated, insistent *"sipp, sipp, sipp…"* which accelerates into an explosive crescendo of trilling; the alternative song is a simple repetition, 10-15 times, of the alarm call, a pure and plaintive *"piu…piu…piu…"*. It also has a *"hooeet"* anxiety call.

The **Goldcrest** is our smallest bird and differs from the leaf warblers in its tiny size, bright crest, miniscule bill and pale wing bars. The beady black eye on a plain-coloured face gives the bird a very different look to the Firecrest (below). Fairly ubiquitous, it is most at home in conifers and other evergreens. Its call (confusable with Tree Creeper, pp. 94-95, and possibly Coal Tit, pp. 112-113) is a very thin *"zee, zee, zee"*. Song is a feeble high-pitched disyllabic note *"tissi"* repeated five to seven times, finishing with a somewhat apologetic descending flourish.

Formerly known only as a spring and autumn migrant, the **Firecrest** is now an expanding, although still rare, breeding species in Britain, mainly in evergreen woodlands where it overlaps with Goldcrest. It can be distinguished from the Goldcrest by the differing head pattern, which is easy to see once the bird is in view. But the most productive way of locating birds in the breeding season (British birds appear to leave breeding areas after nesting) is by their song: lower pitched than Goldcrest, a little harsher and strengthening towards the end. Once the Goldcrest's song is completely learned, listen for the 'similar-but-different' Firecrest. The Firecrest's call is also harder than Goldcrest's: *"zitt"* rather than *"zee"*. Both are agile feeders on the slenderest twigs and can be fairly approachable.

1mm.

Blackcap

Garden Warbler

Garden Warbler: *featureless plumage – an archetypal 'little brown bird' – but monochrome mouse-grey plumage is perhaps actually a helpful distinguishing feature in itself.*

Blackcap *(above): black (male) or brown (female) crown makes identification easy. Some overwinter and can cause confusion with, e.g. Marsh Tit (p. 112) at bird tables.*

Display flight

Whitethroat

♂

The common **Whitethroat** *is a browner bird with rufous edging to wing feathers and has a longer tail than Lesser Whitethroat. Note white eye-ring of common Whitethroat and different leg colour.*

♀

Dartford Warbler

*Dark cap and black ear coverts give a masked appearance to the **Lesser Whitethroat**, which is much greyer than the common Whitethroat and lacks rufous wing feathers. Sexes are alike but male slightly better marked. Very skulking and often difficult to see.*

Lesser Whitethroat

♀

DRY-SCRUB (SYLVIA) WARBLERS

The **Blackcap** and **Garden Warbler** are two of our most accomplished songsters. Both are usually more readily heard than seen as they are skulking birds of deep undergrowth, often reluctant to show themselves (particularly the Garden Warbler). They are somewhat late arrivals (late April onwards). The male Blackcap has a glossy black crown and the female a dark brown crown. Garden Warbler sexes are alike, greyish-brown with no distinctive features. Their songs can be very difficult to separate and to learn. A very accomplished Blackcap is easy enough to distinguish from a mediocre Garden Warbler, but the majority in between are more taxing exercises in identification. Comparisons between song characteristics of the two species are as follows:

Blackcap	Garden Warbler
Remarkably rich and fluting	Same mellow quality without fluty notes
Very varied; lots of sharps and flats	More uniform and even
Shorter phrases	More sustained but lower pitched
Often louder	More subdued
Excellent mimic of other species – including Garden Warbler	
Alarm call a hard "*tac, tac*" and a scolding "*trrrr*"	Alarm "*trrrr*" used more readily than Blackcap; "*tuc*" call is less hard than Blackcap's

The **Whitethroat** is a greyish bird with white chin and 'rusty' wing patch, found in hawthorn scrub, thickets, gorse brakes etc. throughout the British Isles, but scarcer in hill regions of W. and N. The rather similar **Lesser Whitethroat** – greyer with dark, mask-like, ear-coverts – is more strongly south-eastern (completely absent from the uplands of N. and W.) and is typically found as a bird of tall overgrown hedgerows on farmland. Both are skulking birds, the Lesser Whitethroat more so, although the male Whitethroat emerges fairly readily to sing from an exposed spray and also has a short and sudden song flight, towering briefly and plummeting back into cover. Its song is energetic and cheerful, if scratchy. It is a lively, active little bird, plunging in and out of cover with much crest raising and tail cocking. It also raises its crown feathers when agitated or excited. The Lesser Whitethroat's song comprises mainly a tuneless one-note rattle from within the depth of hedgerow cover.

Now confined to a few remnants of heathland in southern England (mostly on nature reserves), the rare **Dartford Warbler** is the only warbler that is wholly resident all year. Dartford Warblers are very dark birds with long tails constantly fanned and cocked. No other British bird resembles it, especially in the restricted gorse and heather areas in which it lives. Extremely skulking, it is usually only seen during brief forays to eminences or flitting across the open from bush to bush. The short scratchy song has a Whitethroat-like quality, sometimes delivered in song flight. The call is a hard, scolding "*tuc...tuc...*".

MARSHLAND WARBLERS AND ALLIES

Reed in Water:
Bearded Tit, Reed Warbler.

Reed with sedge in water:
Savi's Warbler.

Reed Warbler (below left): common in
reed-beds S. Britain; song similar to
Sedge Warbler but more subdued – a
monotonous churring mix of musical
and chattering notes. Often
parasitised by Cuckoos.

Reed Warblers

Marsh
Warbler

*Similar
plumages:
plain upperparts:
check voice and
habitat.*

Marsh Warbler (above): rare
breeder in osier beds, rough
river banks, nettles, southern
England; very musical and
varied song, mimics other
birds. Like Reed Warbler but
paler legs, shorter, stouter
bill; underparts 'cleaner'.

Cetti's Warbler (below):
dense bushy areas by water.
Colonising S. Britain but still
rare. Song is an explosive
"chwee, chwee, chwee"
Rufous upperparts, longish
rounded tail and clear eye-
stripe. Flanks brownish.

Savi's Warbler (below): a few wet reed-
bed sites in S. England. Bulkier than
Reed Warbler; darker underparts and
tail. Song as Grasshopper Warbler but
shorter and lower pitched. Rounded tail.

Reed with carr:
Sedge Warbler, Reed Bunting.

Sedge Warbler (below): energetic,
jumble of melodic and harsh notes, more
ebullient than Reed Warbler: rough
vegetation near water. Streaky plumage,
broad white supercilium, orange rump.

Drier marsh, tangled carr, willow beds:
Cetti's Warbler, Grasshopper Warbler,
Marsh Warbler.

Reed Bunting (below): one of the
commonest and most conspicuous
birds of the reed-bed/scrub
margins. See also pp. 122-123.

Grasshopper Warbler (below):
secretive but has a singular 'song' –
prolonged high-pitched reeling like
distant angler's reel. Wet or dry areas of
rank vegetation. A grey-brown bird with
subdued dark streaking; rounded tail.

Bearded Tit (below): not in fact a
tit, but a babbler. Exclusive to
reed-beds. Look for small rufous
bird with long tail on reed heads
or flying across reed tops. Call is a
twanging "ping, ping".

107

Barred Warblers (above): in autumn, the young are plain ashy coloured with longish tails and heavy bills. Note the staring yellow eye of the adult.

Melodious Warbler (below): note the length of wings relative to the tail compared with Icterine Warbler. The wing does not usually show a pale panel.

Note heavy build of the **Icterine Warbler** (above) compared with leaf warblers (p. 102) and pale panel on closed wing; panel is yellowish in adults, whitish in young birds, but may be missing altogether in worn autumn adults.

Aquatic Warbler (below): beware of confusion in autumn with young Sedge Warblers (below right), which often show a pale crown stripe but never as prominent as the Aquatic Warbler's. Note leg colour (compared to Sedge Warbler) and streaked rump.

Imm.

Barred
Warbler

Adult (⅔ scale)

Icterine
Warbler

Imm.

Melodious Warbler

Yellow-browed
Warbler

Aquatic Warbler

Imm.

Imm.

Sedge Warbler

Among many birds which arrive in Britain 'accidentally' or as scarce passage migrants each year are several warblers. Most arrivals are in autumn and the majority of records, understandably, come from well-watched coastal areas. Many of these birds are young of the year. The five warblers described here are some of those most likely to be encountered among the rarer migrants.

The **Barred Warbler** is a summer visitor to central Europe. Small numbers pass down the E. coast of Britain in Sept.-Oct. and although numbers vary from year to year, it is always scarce. Most individuals are young birds; adults are very rare in Britain. These immature birds have a basic similarity to the Garden Warbler (p. 104) but are larger and more ashy-grey with buffish underparts, longer tails and heavier bills. The forehead often appears steep, as in the Whitethroat (p. 104). Pale edges to the secondaries and tertiaries of these young birds produce an indistinct bar which is visible on the closed wing. White outer tail feathers (unlike Garden Warbler) show particularly in flight. They are skulking and fly close to the ground in the manner of a Dunnock. Barred Warblers have heavy-looking legs and large feet and move about in bushes in a slightly cumbersome manner.

The **Icterine Warbler** breeds in central Europe and Scandinavia and is a scarce autumn migrant in Britain (even scarcer in spring) mainly in the east from Kent to Shetland. Although sharing the green and yellow pattern of the leaf warblers (pp. 102-103), this is a larger, more robust bird with strong bill and bluish-grey legs. The head often has a slightly peaked appearance.

Extremely similar to the Icterine is the **Melodious Warbler**, which replaces it as a breeding bird in southern Europe and is consequently more likely to occur in S. coast counties than on the E. or W. coasts. Both are equally scarce in Britain as passage migrants, and very difficult to separate in the field. The head of the Melodious is rounder and less peaked. The wing is usually unmarked but may show an indistinct yellowish panel on some individuals (see Icterine). The wings are a little shorter than those of the Icterine.

The tiny **Yellow-browed Warbler**, smaller than a Willow Warbler and little bigger than a Goldcrest, is a rare but regular vagrant from Siberia in autumn. Its tiny size, bright supercilium and double whitish wing bars make it easy to identify. As well as feeding among fine twigs and leaves (like Chiffchaff and Willow Warbler) it also makes aerial excursions to chase small insects. Records are mainly from the E. coast in Sept.-Oct. and invariably refer to young birds which are in fresh plumage with underparts showing no yellow. It has a distinctive call – often helpful in locating the bird – an emphatic *"sooeet"*.

The **Aquatic Warbler** (breeds S.E. Europe) is a scarce autumn migrant to Britain, especially S. England (Aug.-Oct.) It is a bird of similar habits and habitat to the Sedge Warbler (p. 107), which it also resembles in plumage but is sandier and has a bold striped head pattern and streaked rump which distinguish it. It is extremely skulking and therefore very difficult to see. The eye-stripe is buffish, not white as in the Sedge Warbler.

Spotted Flycatcher

Spotted Flycatcher (above): the silhouette is noticeably large-headed and large-billed, very different from other flycatchers – or indeed other similar-sized birds. Its perched attitude is erect. It takes large prey (thus the large head and bill) and has grey-brown plumage and a finely streaked breast.

Pied Flycatcher ♂ ♀

The **Pied Flycatcher** (above) has brilliant white underparts when seen from below.

Red-breasted Flycatcher (below): note the pale eye-ring, small size and unique tail pattern.

Pied ♀

Red-breasted Flycatcher

♀

Imm.

Being insectivorous, both our breeding flycatchers – Spotted and Pied – are necessarily summer visitors. The rarer Red-breasted Flycatcher is a drift-migrant (usually in autumn) which breeds in eastern Europe.

The **Spotted Flycatcher** has an undistinguished plumage but a readily recognisable silhouette and characteristic hunting behaviour. Quietly perched on the under branches of a large tree or other similar vantage point, the Spotted Flycatcher sallies out to take fairly large insects (butterflies, hoverflies, bees) on the wing, returning to the same, or a nearby, perch. It flies fast on noticeably long wings, often hovers momentarily or longer, and side-slips or twists with agility. The snap of the mandibles is often audible as it takes the prey. The call is a high single note *"szee"* and the alarm is a repeated rapid *"szee-tuc-tuc"*. Its thin, nondescript apology for a song is – wisely – seldom used and therefore seldom heard. Spotted Flycatchers arrive late, often not until well on into May. They are fairly confiding birds, frequent in gardens and happily nesting on ledges or sills on houses. They are very seldom seen on the ground.

The conspicuous and often confiding **Pied Flycatcher** is a bird of the oakwoods of Wales, northern England and (less densely) parts of Scotland and south-west England; it arrives mid-April. They are not confined to woodland, however, and frequent old hedgerows, gardens, parks and riverside trees. Few are seen in southern or eastern counties in spring but they are more numerous there, especially on coasts, on autumn passage. Pied Flycatchers are active and eye-catching birds, easy to identify. The male's pied plumage is unlike that of any other small British bird, even though individuals vary a lot in the intensity of colouring on the upperparts: the two 'pince-nez' white marks on the forehead are noticeable. The female's patterning is similar to the male's but a warm olive-brown replaces the black of the male's plumage. After the late summer moult, the male closely resembles the female. They are active birds, foraging repeatedly, out from one feeding perch and back to another, and often flicking their wings and flirting their tails. They take to nest boxes more readily than any other woodland bird. The song is a brief but attractive jingle *"tree, tree, tree, peoo, weoo, weeo"* and the anxiety call a single *"witt"* or annoyed *"wi-tik"*.

Red-breasted Flycatchers occur as 'accidental' migrants in autumn, most commonly on the E. coasts of Britain. They nest in eastern Europe and Russia. It is a small 'round' flycatcher, and although the plumage of females and young birds is a little nondescript, the male is readily distinguished by the orange-red throat and grey head, which are diagnostic at all seasons. The females and immatures are duller with mid-brown upperparts and creamy-buff underparts. In all plumages the tail pattern is the definite identification feature. It is blackish with prominent white side panels which are prominent and can be seen easily as the bird frequently flicks and cocks the tail upwards. When perched, the wings are often held in a drooped position. The call is a harsh Wren-like *"chuc"* when alarmed.

Long-tailed Tit

Blue Tit

Listen for **Long-tailed Tit's** (above) frequent contact call – a trilling "pirrup". Parties work along hedgerows, crossing open areas in Indian file.
Great Tit (below) has striking white cheeks, black cap, collar and throat and a black band down centre of underparts.

Blue
Imm

Gre
Imm

Great Tit

There is little risk of confusing the **Blue Tit** (above): the blue tail and blue cap are diagnostic.

The **Crested Tit** (below) is easily identified by unique head patterning and prominent crest.

Coal Tit

The **Coal Tit** (above) has a glossy black head pattern with a white nape stripe and buffish underparts.

Crested Tit

Note the larger black cap and bull-headed appearance of **Willow Tit** (below left) and the sleeker, 'cleaner' form of **Marsh Tit** (below right).

Willow Tit

Marsh Tit

The tiny **Long-tailed Tit** is the only small (6cm/2½″) bird with a tail longer than its body. Common throughout the country, it is most frequently encountered in family parties of 8-12, working along hedgerows or thickets, scrub and woodland edge. Like all tits, it is an acrobatic feeder. In winter, they often join mixed parties of other tits, Goldcrests etc. The only time that the female is likely to be distinguished from the male is in spring when her long tail becomes bent through incubating in the tiny domed nest.

The familiar **Blue Tit** is one of the best known garden birds, making ready use of bird tables and nest boxes. Young birds show varying degrees of yellow on their cheeks well into winter and have greener wing coverts than the clear blue of the adults. Males are brighter than females, especially the blue on the head and wing coverts.

The **Great Tit** – almost a third bigger than the Blue Tit – is equally familiar and easy to identify. A bold black band – wider and blacker in male – runs the length of the underparts from throat to lower belly. Great Tits have a miscellany of calls but the basic elements of the song are a bi-syllabic *"see-saw, see-saw, see-saw…"*

The **Crested Tit** is restricted to mature open pine forests, often with some birch, in N.E. Scotland. It has a very distinctive trilling call which, once recognised, readily locates it. Pairs are often widely scattered. Sexes are virtually indistinguishable in the field.

Marsh Tit and **Willow Tit** are the two members of the family which are extremely similar in plumage and habitat. They are both plain brown with pale cheeks and underparts and black caps. Their differences have to be carefully looked for and they rarely occur together so comparison is difficult. The Marsh Tit is a sleek bird with neat black bib and a crisply defined, shinier black cap. By comparison, the Willow Tit has much looser, fluffier plumage, is larger-headed with a bull-necked appearance, enhanced by the larger matt cap and more extensive bib. The Willow Tit's buffish flanks (Marsh Tit's are uniform greyish-white) are a sounder field character than the frequently cited pale wing patch (which, in any case, is less evident in summer). The difference in calls is important. Marsh Tit's basic call is a strong *"pitt-chu, pitt-chu…"* which is absent from the Willow Tit's repertoire. The Willow Tit's most common and best recognised call is a buzzing *"ti-zurr, zurr, zurr"*. Both are absent from Ireland and rare through most of Scotland. The difference in habitat preference is sometimes helpful: Marsh Tits are primarily birds of open deciduous woodland, being rare in conifers, whereas Willow Tits are happiest among softer woods – conifers, alder, birch or willows – especially in damp situations. In these respects the Marsh Tit's name is an unfortunate misnomer. Marsh Tits come to bird tables in winter; Willow Tits very rarely.

The **Coal Tit** is familiar as a garden bird, especially at feeding tables. Smaller than the Blue Tit, it is most likely to be confused initially with Marsh or Willow Tit, but the small size, warm brown underparts and white spot on the nape readily distinguish it. Although universally distributed, Coal Tits have a predilection for conifer woods. The song is a reedy *"pee-choo, pee-choo…"*.

The Bearded Tit is described and illustrated on page 107.

Carrion Crow

Cawing posture

Imm.

Hooded Crow

Differences in bill shape, face pattern, gait and thigh feathering distinguish the **Carrion Crow** (above) from the Rook. Note square-ended tail (compare Raven). Young Rooks and Carrion Crows are similar.

Rook

Imm.

Rooks (above) have a bluish sheen and slightly more elongated profile than crows. Note the rounded tail.
Raven (below): its aerial evolutions (left) often help to identify it. It is a large, powerful and heavily built bird. Note wedge-shaped tail and big bill.

Raven

The **Carrion Crow** is a very numerous bird and although common and familiar it is not always easy to separate from the Rook or, in hill country, from the Raven. All are jet black birds but in good light the Carrion Crow has a greener sheen than the others. The greatest likelihood of confusion arises with immature Rooks in summer and autumn (see below). Carrion Crows are shy, careful, suspicious and evasive birds, often with a malevolent mien, hunch-shouldered on a perch or slipping surreptitiously out of range or out of sight when disturbed. On the wing it has a level and determined flight with squarish wings (primaries spread as in all crows) and a square-ended tail (compare with Raven). On the ground it walks well, without the Rook's more rolling gait. The bill is shorter than Rook's, feathered to the base and gives a slightly decurved impression. The call is a loud insistent *"kraa"* or *"kraa, kraa, kraa"*. Most usually solitary or in pairs, but flocks can be large in areas where it is numerous, e.g. Wales. Not colonial.

In north-west Scotland, the Isle of Man and Ireland, the birds are the same species but of the **Hooded Crow** variety – a black-winged, black-headed and grey-bodied sub-species. Where the two sub-species meet they interbreed freely and, apart from their plumage colour, Hooded Crows are in every way identical to their all-black congeners.

Rooks are highly gregarious birds, both in their colonial nesting and in their feeding. Although very similar to Carrion Crows in colour, size and habit, there are distinctive differences to look for. The Rook has a bare, grey face and a longer, more pointed bill which, together with a rolling gait, 'baggy' thigh feathering and communal habits, serve to identify it positively. The call is more drawn out and less raucous than a crow's – the familiar 'cawing' associated with the rookeries in spring. On the wing, Rooks have a looser, quicker wing action. Young Rooks do not have bare faces and are more difficult to separate from Carrion Crows; bill shape is then the best factor. Rooks have adapted well to modern conditions and often forage on the sides of busy main roads.

The massive **Raven**, nearly half as big again as a crow, is numerous in south-west England, Wales, and parts of northern England, Scotland and Ireland. It particularly inhabits mountain areas and sea cliffs. Although, at a distance, it may be difficult to distinguish from the Carrion Crow, its flight characteristics and voice often give it away. It is the only member of the crow family to soar habitually and its long wings and powerful wing beats give it a distinctive flight attitude. Even at a distance, the huge head and bill should be evident. Note too the wedge-shaped tail. Ravens are considerable aerial acrobats and frequently roll onto their backs, tumble and dive, often calling as they do so. They have a deep-throated *"prok"* with considerable individual variation from one bird to another. Large congregations of Ravens can occur at good food supplies or favoured tree roosts. Nest sites are traditional, usually on cliffs, but sometimes in trees, and may be used for years on end; in such cases, nests are sometimes very large.

Raven   *Carrion Crow*   *Rook*   *Jackdaw*   *Chough*

Choughs

*The **Chough's** shining black plumage (above), red bill and legs make it easy to identify. In flight it has distinctive silhouettes and a diagnostic ringing call. **Jackdaw** (left): grey nape, silver eye and small size tell it from other crows.*

Jackdaw

*Pied plumage with iridescent green tail and shiny blue wings make the **Magpie** (below) unmistakable.*

*****Jays** (bottom) have a unique combination of pink, blue, black and white although they seldom permit close views. Crest feathers are erected when excited.*

Magpies

Jays

CROWS: SMALLER CROWS

The **Chough** is a bird of the cliff coasts of Wales, the Isle of Man, Mull of Kintyre and Islay as well as the rugged coasts of Ireland. Inland pairs breed in Snowdonia – usually in old mineshafts and quarries – and S.W. Ireland where it uses inland cliffs and derelict buildings. This is a bird of wild windblown cliffs and quarries. Highly aerobatic, birds tumble and cavort in the updraughts, calling noisily and often dropping long distances with wings folded. In level flight the wing tips are clearly upturned and the primaries are widely spread. They feed on grassy ledges and cliff tops where the pillar-box-red legs and bills are easily seen as birds probe energetically at the turf. They are often cheek-by-jowel with the similar-sized Jackdaw but are easily distinguished by flight, call and general behaviour. Juvenile birds have shorter orange bills. The call is a wild, drawn out *"chaaay"* or *"chow"*.

The familiar **Jackdaw** is the smallest of the 'black' crows, two-thirds the size of a Rook. It is common in many towns as well as being plentiful in old woodland, sea cliffs, quarries and old buildings. They frequently nest in unused chimneys filling them with piles of sticks. It is usually best identified by the grey nape, ear coverts and breast set against the black of the remaining plumage. Adults have a striking silver-coloured eye. It is a perky, inquisitive bird which walks on the ground with a jaunty confident air and a business-like manner. It is gregarious and frequently associates with Rooks on farmland. Flocks also forage with gulls and crows on refuse tips. The call notes are fairly clipped: *"chak, chak"* or *"keeak"*. With shorter wings than other crows the flight is quick, almost hurried and primaries are less separated than the other species. Flocks often perform agile aerial manoeuvres.

The **Magpie** is an unmistakable bird with bold pied plumage, long glossy green tail and rounded wings. Although wary of man they are common near habitations and have become increasingly urban. Their harsh chattering call is also distinctive. Magpies build conspicuous domed nests in thorn bushes or high up in trees although, like other crows, they feed mainly on the ground; often they feed on animal road casualties. They move with a combination of easy gait and sidling hops. Although folk rhymes suggest a solitary or paired nature, they are fairly gregarious especially at roosts; parties of up to a dozen are not uncommon and roosts sometimes involve a hundred birds or more. It is absent from much of Scotland and populations are now low in parts of E. England where hedgerow and tree cover is sparse; elsewhere very common.

The **Jay** is a numerous woodland bird but very shy and retiring. Accordingly it is not readily seen at close quarters but most frequently observed flying into cover or passing overhead from one woodland to another. Even then, when its colouring may not be apparent, it is easily recognised by its distinctly slow and floppy flight and the conspicuous white rump patch. When seen in the open the pink body and black moustachial stripe are immediately obvious. Like Magpies they visit gardens to predate on nestling birds and also take peas and soft fruits. Jays have a raucous screaming call but are also excellent mimcs of other large birds, for example Tawny Owl and Buzzard.

Twite
Winter

The **Twite** (above) is a Linnet-like bird but shows less white in wings or tail, lacks red on head or breast and has a streaked buffish throat.

Linnet
Spring ♀

Aut ♂

The amount of red on male **Linnets** (above) varies individually. Note grey head and chestnut mantle. In winter, the crimson areas are hidden by buff fringes to the feathers. Bill colour is pale in summer and dark in winter.

Redpoll
♂ ♀

Male **Redpoll** (above) has a crimson crown and pink flush on the breast. Both sexes have a distinctive little black bib.

♀

Bullfinch

♂

The **Bullfinch's** (above) outline and colour combination are unmistakable.

Hawfinch

The **Hawfinch** (above) has unmistakable outline and patterning but is scarce and often difficult to see.
Goldfinch (below): note red, white and black face pattern and golden wing bars.

Goldfinch

The **Linnet** is a widely distributed finch particularly associated with gorse-grown areas, railway banks and similar rough scrub; in winter they feed with other finches on the ground in open country. Linnets fly with undulating flight and constant twittering calls. In summer the male is a bright bird with a chestnut back, grey head and crimson forehead and breast. Females lack crimson and have much browner streaked plumage including streaked breast. The forked tail and wings are dark with white edgings which show as the bird rises and flies. Most likely confusion is with Redpoll or Twite. However, Twite normally have restricted distribution (see below) and are slenderer with darker upperparts and a more deeply forked tail; note also differing bill colours and call. Redpoll are tiny birds, usually arboreal and have black chins lacking in the Linnet; Linnets feed on the ground.

Twite are moorland breeders, scarce in the Pennines and plentiful in western Ireland, N. and W. Scotland and its islands. They are streaky brown finches with longish forked tails and a distinctive nasal twanging *"chweet"*; flocks also twitter in much the same way as Linnets. When disturbed from feeding in fields or coastal marshes, the parties frequently fly up to perch on wires, fences etc. and indulge in active bill wiping, preening and calling before dropping down to feed again. The dark tail is white-edged but less strongly than Linnet's. In winter, the Twite is the only brown finch to have a pale yellow bill. The male has a pink rump but this is not easy to see in the field.

The **Redpoll** is a tiny brown finch with a wide distribution in different types of woodland, with a preference for birches, alders and new conifer plantations; still increasing in numbers. They are arboreal feeders, often found with Siskins (p. 120) in alders or birches in winter. They are usually most readily identified by the distinctive flight call, a high pitched, rattling *"chi chi chi…"*. Rarer Arctic races of Redpoll may appear occasionally.

The **Bullfinch's** silhouette is of a small 'neckless', bull-headed bird with a very short bill and plump form. The female has similar patterning to the colourful male but with pinkish-brown underparts and brownish back. The eyes are 'invisible' in the black cap, but the pure white rump is an important feature – clearly seen as birds fly into cover. They are somewhat retiring birds of scrub and shrubbery, often located by the soft whistling call note *"pheuu"*.

With heavy head and huge bill, the **Hawfinch** is unmistakable when seen but is actually a very shy and wary bird, often difficult to locate even if it is known to be in the area. The best means of finding it is often to listen for the loud, explosive *"zick"* call. Birds spend a lot of time in tree tops but also feed on the ground on beech mast, sloes etc. It is thinly distributed in England, Wales and southern Scotland but probably considerably overlooked. Sexes are similar but the male is brighter.

The strikingly coloured, easily recognised **Goldfinch** occurs wherever waste ground, roadsides or gardens provide a source of thistles, groundsel, dandelion and other seeds; it is more numerous in summer as many individuals move away in autumn. Sexes similar. The liquid, 'tinkling bell' calls are unmistakable.

♀ Winter

♂

Chaffinch

♂ Spring

Brambling

Winter

♂

Chaffinch (above): the double white wing flashes are much more prominent than any other finch's. Both sexes often show distinctively peaked heads. Male **Crossbill** (below) is bright brick red and the female greyish-green with a yellow rump patch. The **Scottish** and larger **Parrot Crossbill** (below left) have even heavier and deeper bills.

In winter the male **Brambling** is a little brighter than female and has a black-tipped yellow bill. White rump and yellowish underwing show well in flight.

♀

♂

Crossbill

Parrot ♂

Scottish ♀

Siskins (below) often associate with Redpolls in winter. They are the only small birds with black, yellow and green plumage.

♂

♀

Siskin

Serin (right and below): the rump shows yellow in flight.

The **Greenfinch** (above and below) is the largest yellow-green finch, fairly bulky with a powerful bill.

♂

Serin ♀

Greenfinch ♀

The **Chaffinch** is the most numerous British finch, both as a resident and as a winter visitor in large flocks. It breeds throughout the country wherever trees and bushes provide cover. The male is brightly coloured, familiar and unlikely to be confused but the female is drabber and somewhat undistinguished. In flight the double white wing bar is a good feature. The olive green rump shows well on both sexes in flight. Alarm note is a hard, monotonous *"pink, pink"*.

The **Brambling** is a gregarious winter visitor to Britain from the forests of N. Europe. Numbers in winter vary depending on the availability of beech mast crops on the continent. It is somewhat similar to Chaffinch in winter but both sexes have narrow white rumps – visible in flight – and a mottled plumage of oranges, greys, white and black. They are ground feeding birds often associating with Chaffinches, tits or others on the ground below beech trees. The flight call, a rapid repeated *"tchuk, tchuk,"* is completely unlike the Chaffinch's. Birds are rare in summer plumage in this country.

The **Crossbill** is a large bulky finch with a heavy bill and uniquely crossed mandibles. It occurs widely on the mainland of Britain, both as an increasing breeding species (often associated with the new generation of spruce forests) and as an irregular irruptive winter visitor from N. Europe. The birds feed, rather parrot-like, on cone seeds high up in the trees and often leave a litter of spent cones underneath. The flight call is a crisp emphatic *"chip, chip, chip"* which often identifies the birds even when they cannot be seen. Young birds resemble the females but are heavily streaked above and below.

The **Scottish Crossbill** is very similar but with a distinctly heavier bill for dealing with Scots pine cones. It inhabits areas of old Caledonian pine forest in north-east Scotland.

The **Parrot Crossbill**, a larger bird with an even heavier bill, occasionally reaches Britain from north-central Europe and has bred in recent years.

The male **Greenfinch** is a darkish olive-green bird with brighter yellow-green on the breast and rump. Bright yellow markings on wings and tail are most noticeable when the bird takes flight. The female is an overall greyish-brown bird and also has the yellow markings although they are less extensive and duller. The male's twittering song has a terminal drawn out *"swee"*. Greenfinches are widespread in gardens, parks and wooded and shrubby habitats.

Siskins are very small finches, highly acrobatic arboreal feeders with deeply forked tails. The males are a bright mixture of yellows, greens and black while the females are duller and streakier and differ from Redpolls (p. 118) in having touches of yellow and green; often in company with Redpolls in winter. The squeaky *"tsy-zii"* call is distinctive and the male's song is a rapid nasal twittering ending with a drawn-out Greenfinch-like *"swee"*.

The rare **Serin** occurs only locally as a breeding species in southern England. It is the tiniest of finches, the male bright yellow and the female similar but less bright and with poorer head markings. Both sexes have yellow rumps and minute stubby bills. The flight call is a rapid *"see-twee-twee-twee"*.

Yellowhammer

Cirl Bunting

Autumn

Reed Bunting

Spring ♂

The **Yellowhammer** *(above): the only bunting with a chestnut rump. Male's bright head is obvious in summer. Often perches prominently.*

Cirl Bunting *(above): note colour of rump for separation (especially female) from Yellowhammer. Male's head pattern differs from any other bunting.*

The male **Reed Bunting's** *(left) bright head pattern is somewhat obscured in winter. The female shares the distinctive pale collar and moustachial stripe.*

Corn Buntings *(below) are bulky with characteristic head shape and brown-above-and-white-below patterning.*

Corn Bunting

Lapland Bunting *(below) has a nondescript winter plumage; summer male is striking but seldom seen in Britain.*

Snow Buntings *(bottom) are coastal birds in winter. When disturbed they have a clear flickering white pattern in flight.*

Ortolan *(below): note pink bill, yellow throat and pinkish-buff underparts.*

Ortolan

Lapland Bunting

Spring

Winter

Snow Bunting

Winter

Summer ♂

♀ Winter

♂ Winter

The **Yellowhammer** is widespread on farmland, commons and roadsides. Its one note song is delivered from a high song post: *"chi-chi-chi-chi-chi-chi, chweee"* with the last note emphasised and sometimes a little higher (at other times omitted altogether) – traditionally rendered as 'little-bit-of-bread-and-no-cheese'. The male has a canary-yellow head and underparts and a chestnut rump while the female and young are less yellow but still have the chestnut rump. The female has similar head markings to the Cirl Bunting (see below) but rump colours separate the two. The longish tail is frequently flicked: note the white outer feathers. Mixes with other buntings and finches in winter.

The **Cirl Bunting** is a scarce bird restricted to warm slopes and valleys on farmland in southern counties, especially in the south-west. Easily overlooked. The male has a unique head pattern and a black throat (obscured in winter) but is otherwise superficially similar to the Yellowhammer. It has a greenish breast-band and chestnut sides to the breast. Both sexes have an olive-brown rump. The call is a weak *"sship"* and the song a monotonous one-note rattle, similar to Lesser Whitethroat.

The male **Reed Bunting** is unlikely to be mistaken once the black face and throat feathers appear in spring. The black head pattern with white 'moustache' and collar are distinctive. Winter males lose the black markings but the pattern remains; females also show moustachial markings. Males perch prominently and have a monotonous repetitive song *"chip, chip, chip, chippik"*. Reed Buntings are typical of bushy areas on the edge of wetlands (see pp. 106-107) but also occur on drier sites. In winter birds wander farther afield often mixing with finches and other buntings.

The **Corn Bunting** is the largest of the buntings, a heavily built bird brownish above and white below with dark streaking on the throat and sides of the breast. It is a bird of open farmland and coasts but has a discontinuous distribution: few in Wales, Ireland and uplands of N. England and Scotland. Males sing from high prominent song posts, often overhead wires, and have a short distinctive 'jingling key' song, unmusical and dry. Sexes are alike.

The **Ortolan** is a scarce passage visitor, mainly to coastal areas in the S. and E. Both sexes have yellow throats, pale olive-green heads with a distinctive facial pattern, pink bills and pinkish-buff underparts; the male is more strongly coloured and have an olive breast band (female's breast is dark streaked)). It is a very slim looking bunting. Young birds are browner with pink bill and pale eye-ring.

The **Lapland Bunting** is a scarce winter visitor and passage bird. In winter both sexes are somewhat nondescript, similar to female Reed Buntings. Note the pale line through the crown, short tail and stouter form. Lapland Buntings occur mainly in coastal areas, often with Skylarks, Snow Buntings or Shore Larks. The *"Tikki..-tik..teu"* call is distinctive.

Snow Buntings winter in eastern coastal areas, feeding on shingle and sand dunes. Unobtrusive birds, they fly at the last moment and then have eye-catching black-and-white patterns, dancing flight and tinkling *"peu"* calls. A few pairs breed in the Scottish Highlands.

SPARROWS, DUNNOCK STARLING

House Sparrow

Spring ♂

♀

Winter ♂

Dunnock

The **Dunnock** (above) is numerous but unobtrusive, largely a ground dweller. Although dun-coloured, the plumage is in fact warm and delicately patterned. Flicks tail and wings constantly.

The abundant and familiar **House Sparrow** (above) needs little introduction. The male has a grey crown and black bib. The plainer female has a pale eye-stripe. They share the white wing bar.

Tree Sparrow

The **Tree Sparrow** (above and right) is smaller and neater than House. Sexes alike with chocolate brown crowns, white neck-collar, black cheek patch. Uncommon in wooded hedgerows: often with finch flocks in winter. Scarce in N. Scotland and Ireland.

Starling (below): in spring bright and iridescent; more spangled in winter.

Starling

Spring

Summer

Imm.

Winter

INDEX

Page references in bold type indicate the main illustration reference; in all cases, the main text reference will be found on the facing page, or, in a few cases, in the form of a caption, on the same page. References in italic are to subsidiary illustrations; references in normal type indicate a subsidiary text reference. Where the generic name has been abbreviated to a single capital letter, genus is the same as in the entry directly preceding it.

OTHER BIRD BOOKS FROM COLLINS

THE BIRDS OF BRITAIN AND EUROPE
With North Africa and the Middle East *(Revised Edition)*
Hermann Heinzel, Richard Fitter and John Parslow

ISBN 0 00 219210 1

A FIELD GUIDE TO THE BIRDS OF BRITAIN AND EUROPE
(New Edition)
Roger Peterson, Guy Mountfort and P.A.D. Hollom

ISBN 0 00 219073 7

COLLINS BIRD GUIDE
G. Stuart Keith and John Gooders

ISBN 0 00 219119 9

COLLINS BRITISH BIRDS
Terence Lambert and John Gooders

ISBN 0 00 219121 0

THE COMPLETE GUIDE TO BRITISH WILDLIFE
Norman Arlott, Alastair Fitter and Richard Fitter

ISBN 0 00 219212 8

A FIELD GUIDE TO THE SEABIRDS OF BRITAIN AND THE WORLD
Gerald Tuck and Hermann Heinzel

ISBN 0 00 219286 1

ATLAS OF THE BIRDS OF THE WESTERN PALAEARCTIC
Colin Harrison

ISBN 0 00 219729 4